C-1796   CAREER EXAMINATION SERIES

This is your
PASSBOOK for...

Medical Clerk

Test Preparation Study Guide
Questions & Answers

COPYRIGHT NOTICE

This book is SOLELY intended for, is sold ONLY to, and its use is RESTRICTED to individual, bona fide applicants or candidates who qualify by virtue of having seriously filed applications for appropriate license, certificate, professional and/or promotional advancement, higher school matriculation, scholarship, or other legitimate requirements of education and/or governmental authorities.

This book is NOT intended for use, class instruction, tutoring, training, duplication, copying, reprinting, excerption, or adaptation, etc., by:

1) Other publishers
2) Proprietors and/or Instructors of "Coaching" and/or Preparatory Courses
3) Personnel and/or Training Divisions of commercial, industrial, and governmental organizations
4) Schools, colleges, or universities and/or their departments and staffs, including teachers and other personnel
5) Testing Agencies or Bureaus
6) Study groups which seek by the purchase of a single volume to copy and/or duplicate and/or adapt this material for use by the group as a whole without having purchased individual volumes for each of the members of the group
7) Et al.

Such persons would be in violation of appropriate Federal and State statutes.

PROVISION OF LICENSING AGREEMENTS – Recognized educational, commercial, industrial, and governmental institutions and organizations, and others legitimately engaged in educational pursuits, including training, testing, and measurement activities, may address request for a licensing agreement to the copyright owners, who will determine whether, and under what conditions, including fees and charges, the materials in this book may be used them. In other words, a licensing facility exists for the legitimate use of the material in this book on other than an individual basis. However, it is asseverated and affirmed here that the material in this book CANNOT be used without the receipt of the express permission of such a licensing agreement from the Publishers. Inquiries re licensing should be addressed to the company, attention rights and permissions department.

All rights reserved, including the right of reproduction in whole or in part, in any form or by any means, electronic or mechanical, including photocopying, recording, or by any information storage and retrieval system, without permission in writing from the Publisher.

Copyright © 2025 by
National Learning Corporation

212 Michael Drive, Syosset, NY 11791
(516) 921-8888 • www.passbooks.com
E-mail: info@passbooks.com

PASSBOOK® SERIES

THE *PASSBOOK® SERIES* has been created to prepare applicants and candidates for the ultimate academic battlefield – the examination room.

At some time in our lives, each and every one of us may be required to take an examination – for validation, matriculation, admission, qualification, registration, certification, or licensure.

Based on the assumption that every applicant or candidate has met the basic formal educational standards, has taken the required number of courses, and read the necessary texts, the *PASSBOOK® SERIES* furnishes the one special preparation which may assure passing with confidence, instead of failing with insecurity. Examination questions – together with answers – are furnished as the basic vehicle for study so that the mysteries of the examination and its compounding difficulties may be eliminated or diminished by a sure method.

This book is meant to help you pass your examination provided that you qualify and are serious in your objective.

The entire field is reviewed through the huge store of content information which is succinctly presented through a provocative and challenging approach – the question-and-answer method.

A climate of success is established by furnishing the correct answers at the end of each test.

You soon learn to recognize types of questions, forms of questions, and patterns of questioning. You may even begin to anticipate expected outcomes.

You perceive that many questions are repeated or adapted so that you can gain acute insights, which may enable you to score many sure points.

You learn how to confront new questions, or types of questions, and to attack them confidently and work out the correct answers.

You note objectives and emphases, and recognize pitfalls and dangers, so that you may make positive educational adjustments.

Moreover, you are kept fully informed in relation to new concepts, methods, practices, and directions in the field.

You discover that you are actually taking the examination all the time: you are preparing for the examination by "taking" an examination, not by reading extraneous and/or supererogatory textbooks.

In short, this PASSBOOK®, used directedly, should be an important factor in helping you to pass your test.

MEDICAL CLERK

DUTIES
This work involves the responsibility for performing specialized clerical work of medical character dealing with various programs. The specific duties of an incumbent will vary according to the assigned program area and can include such responsibilities as obtaining client information and receiving agency referrals, verifying client eligibility for services, and performing other related secretarial and clerical duties that involve typing. The work is performed under general supervision in accordance with established policies and procedures. May supervise other clerical staff when necessary. Does related work as required.

SCOPE OF THE EXAMINATION
The written test will cover knowledge, skills and/or abilities in such areas as:

1. Office record keeping;
2. Understanding and interpreting written material;
3. Name and number checking; and
4. Medical terminology.

HOW TO TAKE A TEST

I. YOU MUST PASS AN EXAMINATION

A. *WHAT EVERY CANDIDATE SHOULD KNOW*

Examination applicants often ask us for help in preparing for the written test. What can I study in advance? What kinds of questions will be asked? How will the test be given? How will the papers be graded?

As an applicant for a civil service examination, you may be wondering about some of these things. Our purpose here is to suggest effective methods of advance study and to describe civil service examinations.

Your chances for success on this examination can be increased if you know how to prepare. Those "pre-examination jitters" can be reduced if you know what to expect. You can even experience an adventure in good citizenship if you know why civil service exams are given.

B. *WHY ARE CIVIL SERVICE EXAMINATIONS GIVEN?*

Civil service examinations are important to you in two ways. As a citizen, you want public jobs filled by employees who know how to do their work. As a job seeker, you want a fair chance to compete for that job on an equal footing with other candidates. The best-known means of accomplishing this two-fold goal is the competitive examination.

Exams are widely publicized throughout the nation. They may be administered for jobs in federal, state, city, municipal, town or village governments or agencies.

Any citizen may apply, with some limitations, such as the age or residence of applicants. Your experience and education may be reviewed to see whether you meet the requirements for the particular examination. When these requirements exist, they are reasonable and applied consistently to all applicants. Thus, a competitive examination may cause you some uneasiness now, but it is your privilege and safeguard.

C. *HOW ARE CIVIL SERVICE EXAMS DEVELOPED?*

Examinations are carefully written by trained technicians who are specialists in the field known as "psychological measurement," in consultation with recognized authorities in the field of work that the test will cover. These experts recommend the subject matter areas or skills to be tested; only those knowledges or skills important to your success on the job are included. The most reliable books and source materials available are used as references. Together, the experts and technicians judge the difficulty level of the questions.

Test technicians know how to phrase questions so that the problem is clearly stated. Their ethics do not permit "trick" or "catch" questions. Questions may have been tried out on sample groups, or subjected to statistical analysis, to determine their usefulness.

Written tests are often used in combination with performance tests, ratings of training and experience, and oral interviews. All of these measures combine to form the best-known means of finding the right person for the right job.

II. HOW TO PASS THE WRITTEN TEST

A. NATURE OF THE EXAMINATION

To prepare intelligently for civil service examinations, you should know how they differ from school examinations you have taken. In school you were assigned certain definite pages to read or subjects to cover. The examination questions were quite detailed and usually emphasized memory. Civil service exams, on the other hand, try to discover your present ability to perform the duties of a position, plus your potentiality to learn these duties. In other words, a civil service exam attempts to predict how successful you will be. Questions cover such a broad area that they cannot be as minute and detailed as school exam questions.

In the public service similar kinds of work, or positions, are grouped together in one "class." This process is known as *position-classification*. All the positions in a class are paid according to the salary range for that class. One class title covers all of these positions, and they are all tested by the same examination.

B. FOUR BASIC STEPS

1) Study the announcement

How, then, can you know what subjects to study? Our best answer is: "Learn as much as possible about the class of positions for which you've applied." The exam will test the knowledge, skills and abilities needed to do the work.

Your most valuable source of information about the position you want is the official exam announcement. This announcement lists the training and experience qualifications. Check these standards and apply only if you come reasonably close to meeting them.

The brief description of the position in the examination announcement offers some clues to the subjects which will be tested. Think about the job itself. Review the duties in your mind. Can you perform them, or are there some in which you are rusty? Fill in the blank spots in your preparation.

Many jurisdictions preview the written test in the exam announcement by including a section called "Knowledge and Abilities Required," "Scope of the Examination," or some similar heading. Here you will find out specifically what fields will be tested.

2) Review your own background

Once you learn in general what the position is all about, and what you need to know to do the work, ask yourself which subjects you already know fairly well and which need improvement. You may wonder whether to concentrate on improving your strong areas or on building some background in your fields of weakness. When the announcement has specified "some knowledge" or "considerable knowledge," or has used adjectives like "beginning principles of…" or "advanced … methods," you can get a clue as to the number and difficulty of questions to be asked in any given field. More questions, and hence broader coverage, would be included for those subjects which are more important in the work. Now weigh your strengths and weaknesses against the job requirements and prepare accordingly.

3) Determine the level of the position

Another way to tell how intensively you should prepare is to understand the level of the job for which you are applying. Is it the entering level? In other words, is this the position in which beginners in a field of work are hired? Or is it an intermediate or advanced level? Sometimes this is indicated by such words as "Junior" or "Senior" in the class title. Other jurisdictions use Roman numerals to designate the level – Clerk I, Clerk II, for example. The word "Supervisor" sometimes appears in the title. If the level is not indicated by the title, check the description of duties. Will you be working under very close supervision, or will you have responsibility for independent decisions in this work?

4) Choose appropriate study materials

Now that you know the subjects to be examined and the relative amount of each subject to be covered, you can choose suitable study materials. For beginning level jobs, or even advanced ones, if you have a pronounced weakness in some aspect of your training, read a modern, standard textbook in that field. Be sure it is up to date and has general coverage. Such books are normally available at your library, and the librarian will be glad to help you locate one. For entry-level positions, questions of appropriate difficulty are chosen – neither highly advanced questions, nor those too simple. Such questions require careful thought but not advanced training.

If the position for which you are applying is technical or advanced, you will read more advanced, specialized material. If you are already familiar with the basic principles of your field, elementary textbooks would waste your time. Concentrate on advanced textbooks and technical periodicals. Think through the concepts and review difficult problems in your field.

These are all general sources. You can get more ideas on your own initiative, following these leads. For example, training manuals and publications of the government agency which employs workers in your field can be useful, particularly for technical and professional positions. A letter or visit to the government department involved may result in more specific study suggestions, and certainly will provide you with a more definite idea of the exact nature of the position you are seeking.

III. KINDS OF TESTS

Tests are used for purposes other than measuring knowledge and ability to perform specified duties. For some positions, it is equally important to test ability to make adjustments to new situations or to profit from training. In others, basic mental abilities not dependent on information are essential. Questions which test these things may not appear as pertinent to the duties of the position as those which test for knowledge and information. Yet they are often highly important parts of a fair examination. For very general questions, it is almost impossible to help you direct your study efforts. What we can do is to point out some of the more common of these general abilities needed in public service positions and describe some typical questions.

1) General information

Broad, general information has been found useful for predicting job success in some kinds of work. This is tested in a variety of ways, from vocabulary lists to questions about current events. Basic background in some field of work, such as sociology or economics, may be sampled in a group of questions. Often these are principles which have become familiar to most persons through exposure rather than through formal training. It is difficult to advise you how to study for these questions; being alert to the world around you is our best suggestion.

2) Verbal ability

An example of an ability needed in many positions is verbal or language ability. Verbal ability is, in brief, the ability to use and understand words. Vocabulary and grammar tests are typical measures of this ability. Reading comprehension or paragraph interpretation questions are common in many kinds of civil service tests. You are given a paragraph of written material and asked to find its central meaning.

3) Numerical ability
Number skills can be tested by the familiar arithmetic problem, by checking paired lists of numbers to see which are alike and which are different, or by interpreting charts and graphs. In the latter test, a graph may be printed in the test booklet which you are asked to use as the basis for answering questions.

4) Observation
A popular test for law-enforcement positions is the observation test. A picture is shown to you for several minutes, then taken away. Questions about the picture test your ability to observe both details and larger elements.

5) Following directions
In many positions in the public service, the employee must be able to carry out written instructions dependably and accurately. You may be given a chart with several columns, each column listing a variety of information. The questions require you to carry out directions involving the information given in the chart.

6) Skills and aptitudes
Performance tests effectively measure some manual skills and aptitudes. When the skill is one in which you are trained, such as typing or shorthand, you can practice. These tests are often very much like those given in business school or high school courses. For many of the other skills and aptitudes, however, no short-time preparation can be made. Skills and abilities natural to you or that you have developed throughout your lifetime are being tested.

Many of the general questions just described provide all the data needed to answer the questions and ask you to use your reasoning ability to find the answers. Your best preparation for these tests, as well as for tests of facts and ideas, is to be at your physical and mental best. You, no doubt, have your own methods of getting into an exam-taking mood and keeping "in shape." The next section lists some ideas on this subject.

IV. KINDS OF QUESTIONS

Only rarely is the "essay" question, which you answer in narrative form, used in civil service tests. Civil service tests are usually of the short-answer type. Full instructions for answering these questions will be given to you at the examination. But in case this is your first experience with short-answer questions and separate answer sheets, here is what you need to know:

1) **Multiple-choice Questions**
Most popular of the short-answer questions is the "multiple choice" or "best answer" question. It can be used, for example, to test for factual knowledge, ability to solve problems or judgment in meeting situations found at work.
A multiple-choice question is normally one of three types—
- It can begin with an incomplete statement followed by several possible endings. You are to find the one ending which *best* completes the statement, although some of the others may not be entirely wrong.
- It can also be a complete statement in the form of a question which is answered by choosing one of the statements listed.

- It can be in the form of a problem – again you select the best answer.

Here is an example of a multiple-choice question with a discussion which should give you some clues as to the method for choosing the right answer:

When an employee has a complaint about his assignment, the action which will *best* help him overcome his difficulty is to
- A. discuss his difficulty with his coworkers
- B. take the problem to the head of the organization
- C. take the problem to the person who gave him the assignment
- D. say nothing to anyone about his complaint

In answering this question, you should study each of the choices to find which is best. Consider choice "A" – Certainly an employee may discuss his complaint with fellow employees, but no change or improvement can result, and the complaint remains unresolved. Choice "B" is a poor choice since the head of the organization probably does not know what assignment you have been given, and taking your problem to him is known as "going over the head" of the supervisor. The supervisor, or person who made the assignment, is the person who can clarify it or correct any injustice. Choice "C" is, therefore, correct. To say nothing, as in choice "D," is unwise. Supervisors have and interest in knowing the problems employees are facing, and the employee is seeking a solution to his problem.

2) True/False Questions

The "true/false" or "right/wrong" form of question is sometimes used. Here a complete statement is given. Your job is to decide whether the statement is right or wrong.

SAMPLE: A roaming cell-phone call to a nearby city costs less than a non-roaming call to a distant city.

This statement is wrong, or false, since roaming calls are more expensive.

This is not a complete list of all possible question forms, although most of the others are variations of these common types. You will always get complete directions for answering questions. Be sure you understand *how* to mark your answers – ask questions until you do.

V. RECORDING YOUR ANSWERS

Computer terminals are used more and more today for many different kinds of exams.

For an examination with very few applicants, you may be told to record your answers in the test booklet itself. Separate answer sheets are much more common. If this separate answer sheet is to be scored by machine – and this is often the case – it is highly important that you mark your answers correctly in order to get credit.

An electronic scoring machine is often used in civil service offices because of the speed with which papers can be scored. Machine-scored answer sheets must be marked with a pencil, which will be given to you. This pencil has a high graphite content which responds to the electronic scoring machine. As a matter of fact, stray dots may register as answers, so do not let your pencil rest on the answer sheet while you are pondering the correct answer. Also, if your pencil lead breaks or is otherwise defective, ask for another.

Since the answer sheet will be dropped in a slot in the scoring machine, be careful not to bend the corners or get the paper crumpled.

The answer sheet normally has five vertical columns of numbers, with 30 numbers to a column. These numbers correspond to the question numbers in your test booklet. After each number, going across the page are four or five pairs of dotted lines. These short dotted lines have small letters or numbers above them. The first two pairs may also have a "T" or "F" above the letters. This indicates that the first two pairs only are to be used if the questions are of the true-false type. If the questions are multiple choice, disregard the "T" and "F" and pay attention only to the small letters or numbers.

Answer your questions in the manner of the sample that follows:

32. The largest city in the United States is
    A. Washington, D.C.
    B. New York City
    C. Chicago
    D. Detroit
    E. San Francisco

1) Choose the answer you think is best. (New York City is the largest, so "B" is correct.)
2) Find the row of dotted lines numbered the same as the question you are answering. (Find row number 32)
3) Find the pair of dotted lines corresponding to the answer. (Find the pair of lines under the mark "B.")
4) Make a solid black mark between the dotted lines.

VI. BEFORE THE TEST

Common sense will help you find procedures to follow to get ready for an examination. Too many of us, however, overlook these sensible measures. Indeed, nervousness and fatigue have been found to be the most serious reasons why applicants fail to do their best on civil service tests. Here is a list of reminders:

- Begin your preparation early – Don't wait until the last minute to go scurrying around for books and materials or to find out what the position is all about.
- Prepare continuously – An hour a night for a week is better than an all-night cram session. This has been definitely established. What is more, a night a week for a month will return better dividends than crowding your study into a shorter period of time.
- Locate the place of the exam – You have been sent a notice telling you when and where to report for the examination. If the location is in a different town or otherwise unfamiliar to you, it would be well to inquire the best route and learn something about the building.
- Relax the night before the test – Allow your mind to rest. Do not study at all that night. Plan some mild recreation or diversion; then go to bed early and get a good night's sleep.
- Get up early enough to make a leisurely trip to the place for the test – This way unforeseen events, traffic snarls, unfamiliar buildings, etc. will not upset you.
- Dress comfortably – A written test is not a fashion show. You will be known by number and not by name, so wear something comfortable.

- Leave excess paraphernalia at home – Shopping bags and odd bundles will get in your way. You need bring only the items mentioned in the official notice you received; usually everything you need is provided. Do not bring reference books to the exam. They will only confuse those last minutes and be taken away from you when in the test room.
- Arrive somewhat ahead of time – If because of transportation schedules you must get there very early, bring a newspaper or magazine to take your mind off yourself while waiting.
- Locate the examination room – When you have found the proper room, you will be directed to the seat or part of the room where you will sit. Sometimes you are given a sheet of instructions to read while you are waiting. Do not fill out any forms until you are told to do so; just read them and be prepared.
- Relax and prepare to listen to the instructions
- If you have any physical problem that may keep you from doing your best, be sure to tell the test administrator. If you are sick or in poor health, you really cannot do your best on the exam. You can come back and take the test some other time.

VII. AT THE TEST

The day of the test is here and you have the test booklet in your hand. The temptation to get going is very strong. Caution! There is more to success than knowing the right answers. You must know how to identify your papers and understand variations in the type of short-answer question used in this particular examination. Follow these suggestions for maximum results from your efforts:

1) Cooperate with the monitor
The test administrator has a duty to create a situation in which you can be as much at ease as possible. He will give instructions, tell you when to begin, check to see that you are marking your answer sheet correctly, and so on. He is not there to guard you, although he will see that your competitors do not take unfair advantage. He wants to help you do your best.

2) Listen to all instructions
Don't jump the gun! Wait until you understand all directions. In most civil service tests you get more time than you need to answer the questions. So don't be in a hurry. Read each word of instructions until you clearly understand the meaning. Study the examples, listen to all announcements and follow directions. Ask questions if you do not understand what to do.

3) Identify your papers
Civil service exams are usually identified by number only. You will be assigned a number; you must not put your name on your test papers. Be sure to copy your number correctly. Since more than one exam may be given, copy your exact examination title.

4) Plan your time
Unless you are told that a test is a "speed" or "rate of work" test, speed itself is usually not important. Time enough to answer all the questions will be provided, but this does not mean that you have all day. An overall time limit has been set. Divide the total time (in minutes) by the number of questions to determine the approximate time you have for each question.

5) Do not linger over difficult questions

If you come across a difficult question, mark it with a paper clip (useful to have along) and come back to it when you have been through the booklet. One caution if you do this – be sure to skip a number on your answer sheet as well. Check often to be sure that you have not lost your place and that you are marking in the row numbered the same as the question you are answering.

6) Read the questions

Be sure you know what the question asks! Many capable people are unsuccessful because they failed to *read* the questions correctly.

7) Answer all questions

Unless you have been instructed that a penalty will be deducted for incorrect answers, it is better to guess than to omit a question.

8) Speed tests

It is often better NOT to guess on speed tests. It has been found that on timed tests people are tempted to spend the last few seconds before time is called in marking answers at random – without even reading them – in the hope of picking up a few extra points. To discourage this practice, the instructions may warn you that your score will be "corrected" for guessing. That is, a penalty will be applied. The incorrect answers will be deducted from the correct ones, or some other penalty formula will be used.

9) Review your answers

If you finish before time is called, go back to the questions you guessed or omitted to give them further thought. Review other answers if you have time.

10) Return your test materials

If you are ready to leave before others have finished or time is called, take ALL your materials to the monitor and leave quietly. Never take any test material with you. The monitor can discover whose papers are not complete, and taking a test booklet may be grounds for disqualification.

VIII. EXAMINATION TECHNIQUES

1) Read the general instructions carefully. These are usually printed on the first page of the exam booklet. As a rule, these instructions refer to the timing of the examination; the fact that you should not start work until the signal and must stop work at a signal, etc. If there are any *special* instructions, such as a choice of questions to be answered, make sure that you note this instruction carefully.

2) When you are ready to start work on the examination, that is as soon as the signal has been given, read the instructions to each question booklet, underline any key words or phrases, such as *least, best, outline, describe* and the like. In this way you will tend to answer as requested rather than discover on reviewing your paper that you *listed without describing*, that you selected the *worst* choice rather than the *best* choice, etc.

3) If the examination is of the objective or multiple-choice type – that is, each question will also give a series of possible answers: A, B, C or D, and you are called upon to select the best answer and write the letter next to that answer on your answer paper – it is advisable to start answering each question in turn. There may be anywhere from 50 to 100 such questions in the three or four hours allotted and you can see how much time would be taken if you read through all the questions before beginning to answer any. Furthermore, if you come across a question or group of questions which you know would be difficult to answer, it would undoubtedly affect your handling of all the other questions.

4) If the examination is of the essay type and contains but a few questions, it is a moot point as to whether you should read all the questions before starting to answer any one. Of course, if you are given a choice – say five out of seven and the like – then it is essential to read all the questions so you can eliminate the two that are most difficult. If, however, you are asked to answer all the questions, there may be danger in trying to answer the easiest one first because you may find that you will spend too much time on it. The best technique is to answer the first question, then proceed to the second, etc.

5) Time your answers. Before the exam begins, write down the time it started, then add the time allowed for the examination and write down the time it must be completed, then divide the time available somewhat as follows:
    - If 3-1/2 hours are allowed, that would be 210 minutes. If you have 80 objective-type questions, that would be an average of 2-1/2 minutes per question. Allow yourself no more than 2 minutes per question, or a total of 160 minutes, which will permit about 50 minutes to review.
    - If for the time allotment of 210 minutes there are 7 essay questions to answer, that would average about 30 minutes a question. Give yourself only 25 minutes per question so that you have about 35 minutes to review.

6) The most important instruction is to *read each question* and make sure you know what is wanted. The second most important instruction is to *time yourself properly* so that you answer every question. The third most important instruction is to *answer every question*. Guess if you have to but include something for each question. Remember that you will receive no credit for a blank and will probably receive some credit if you write something in answer to an essay question. If you guess a letter – say "B" for a multiple-choice question – you may have guessed right. If you leave a blank as an answer to a multiple-choice question, the examiners may respect your feelings but it will not add a point to your score. Some exams may penalize you for wrong answers, so in such cases *only*, you may not want to guess unless you have some basis for your answer.

7) Suggestions
    a. Objective-type questions
        1. Examine the question booklet for proper sequence of pages and questions
        2. Read all instructions carefully
        3. Skip any question which seems too difficult; return to it after all other questions have been answered
        4. Apportion your time properly; do not spend too much time on any single question or group of questions

5. Note and underline key words – *all, most, fewest, least, best, worst, same, opposite,* etc.
6. Pay particular attention to negatives
7. Note unusual option, e.g., unduly long, short, complex, different or similar in content to the body of the question
8. Observe the use of "hedging" words – *probably, may, most likely,* etc.
9. Make sure that your answer is put next to the same number as the question
10. Do not second-guess unless you have good reason to believe the second answer is definitely more correct
11. Cross out original answer if you decide another answer is more accurate; do not erase until you are ready to hand your paper in
12. Answer all questions; guess unless instructed otherwise
13. Leave time for review

   b. Essay questions
1. Read each question carefully
2. Determine exactly what is wanted. Underline key words or phrases.
3. Decide on outline or paragraph answer
4. Include many different points and elements unless asked to develop any one or two points or elements
5. Show impartiality by giving pros and cons unless directed to select one side only
6. Make and write down any assumptions you find necessary to answer the questions
7. Watch your English, grammar, punctuation and choice of words
8. Time your answers; don't crowd material

8) Answering the essay question

Most essay questions can be answered by framing the specific response around several key words or ideas. Here are a few such key words or ideas:

M's: manpower, materials, methods, money, management
P's: purpose, program, policy, plan, procedure, practice, problems, pitfalls, personnel, public relations

   a. Six basic steps in handling problems:
1. Preliminary plan and background development
2. Collect information, data and facts
3. Analyze and interpret information, data and facts
4. Analyze and develop solutions as well as make recommendations
5. Prepare report and sell recommendations
6. Install recommendations and follow up effectiveness

   b. Pitfalls to avoid
1. *Taking things for granted* – A statement of the situation does not necessarily imply that each of the elements is necessarily true; for example, a complaint may be invalid and biased so that all that can be taken for granted is that a complaint has been registered

2. *Considering only one side of a situation* – Wherever possible, indicate several alternatives and then point out the reasons you selected the best one
3. *Failing to indicate follow up* – Whenever your answer indicates action on your part, make certain that you will take proper follow-up action to see how successful your recommendations, procedures or actions turn out to be
4. *Taking too long in answering any single question* – Remember to time your answers properly

IX. AFTER THE TEST

Scoring procedures differ in detail among civil service jurisdictions although the general principles are the same. Whether the papers are hand-scored or graded by machine we have described, they are nearly always graded by number. That is, the person who marks the paper knows only the number – never the name – of the applicant. Not until all the papers have been graded will they be matched with names. If other tests, such as training and experience or oral interview ratings have been given, scores will be combined. Different parts of the examination usually have different weights. For example, the written test might count 60 percent of the final grade, and a rating of training and experience 40 percent. In many jurisdictions, veterans will have a certain number of points added to their grades.

After the final grade has been determined, the names are placed in grade order and an eligible list is established. There are various methods for resolving ties between those who get the same final grade – probably the most common is to place first the name of the person whose application was received first. Job offers are made from the eligible list in the order the names appear on it. You will be notified of your grade and your rank as soon as all these computations have been made. This will be done as rapidly as possible.

People who are found to meet the requirements in the announcement are called "eligibles." Their names are put on a list of eligible candidates. An eligible's chances of getting a job depend on how high he stands on this list and how fast agencies are filling jobs from the list.

When a job is to be filled from a list of eligibles, the agency asks for the names of people on the list of eligibles for that job. When the civil service commission receives this request, it sends to the agency the names of the three people highest on this list. Or, if the job to be filled has specialized requirements, the office sends the agency the names of the top three persons who meet these requirements from the general list.

The appointing officer makes a choice from among the three people whose names were sent to him. If the selected person accepts the appointment, the names of the others are put back on the list to be considered for future openings.

That is the rule in hiring from all kinds of eligible lists, whether they are for typist, carpenter, chemist, or something else. For every vacancy, the appointing officer has his choice of any one of the top three eligibles on the list. This explains why the person whose name is on top of the list sometimes does not get an appointment when some of the persons lower on the list do. If the appointing officer chooses the second or third eligible, the No. 1 eligible does not get a job at once, but stays on the list until he is appointed or the list is terminated.

X. HOW TO PASS THE INTERVIEW TEST

The examination for which you applied requires an oral interview test. You have already taken the written test and you are now being called for the interview test – the final part of the formal examination.

You may think that it is not possible to prepare for an interview test and that there are no procedures to follow during an interview. Our purpose is to point out some things you can do in advance that will help you and some good rules to follow and pitfalls to avoid while you are being interviewed.

What is an interview supposed to test?

The written examination is designed to test the technical knowledge and competence of the candidate; the oral is designed to evaluate intangible qualities, not readily measured otherwise, and to establish a list showing the relative fitness of each candidate – as measured against his competitors – for the position sought. Scoring is not on the basis of "right" and "wrong," but on a sliding scale of values ranging from "not passable" to "outstanding." As a matter of fact, it is possible to achieve a relatively low score without a single "incorrect" answer because of evident weakness in the qualities being measured.

Occasionally, an examination may consist entirely of an oral test – either an individual or a group oral. In such cases, information is sought concerning the technical knowledges and abilities of the candidate, since there has been no written examination for this purpose. More commonly, however, an oral test is used to supplement a written examination.

Who conducts interviews?

The composition of oral boards varies among different jurisdictions. In nearly all, a representative of the personnel department serves as chairman. One of the members of the board may be a representative of the department in which the candidate would work. In some cases, "outside experts" are used, and, frequently, a businessman or some other representative of the general public is asked to serve. Labor and management or other special groups may be represented. The aim is to secure the services of experts in the appropriate field.

However the board is composed, it is a good idea (and not at all improper or unethical) to ascertain in advance of the interview who the members are and what groups they represent. When you are introduced to them, you will have some idea of their backgrounds and interests, and at least you will not stutter and stammer over their names.

What should be done before the interview?

While knowledge about the board members is useful and takes some of the surprise element out of the interview, there is other preparation which is more substantive. It *is* possible to prepare for an oral interview – in several ways:

1) Keep a copy of your application and review it carefully before the interview

This may be the only document before the oral board, and the starting point of the interview. Know what education and experience you have listed there, and the sequence and dates of all of it. Sometimes the board will ask you to review the highlights of your experience for them; you should not have to hem and haw doing it.

2) Study the class specification and the examination announcement

Usually, the oral board has one or both of these to guide them. The qualities, characteristics or knowledges required by the position sought are stated in these documents. They offer valuable clues as to the nature of the oral interview. For example, if the job involves supervisory responsibilities, the announcement will usually indicate that knowledge of modern supervisory methods and the qualifications of the candidate as a supervisor will be tested. If so, you can expect such questions, frequently in the form of a hypothetical situation which you are expected to solve. NEVER go into an oral without knowledge of the duties and responsibilities of the job you seek.

3) Think through each qualification required

Try to visualize the kind of questions you would ask if you were a board member. How well could you answer them? Try especially to appraise your own knowledge and background in each area, *measured against the job sought*, and identify any areas in which you are weak. Be critical and realistic – do not flatter yourself.

4) Do some general reading in areas in which you feel you may be weak

For example, if the job involves supervision and your past experience has NOT, some general reading in supervisory methods and practices, particularly in the field of human relations, might be useful. Do NOT study agency procedures or detailed manuals. The oral board will be testing your understanding and capacity, not your memory.

5) Get a good night's sleep and watch your general health and mental attitude

You will want a clear head at the interview. Take care of a cold or any other minor ailment, and of course, no hangovers.

What should be done on the day of the interview?

Now comes the day of the interview itself. Give yourself plenty of time to get there. Plan to arrive somewhat ahead of the scheduled time, particularly if your appointment is in the fore part of the day. If a previous candidate fails to appear, the board might be ready for you a bit early. By early afternoon an oral board is almost invariably behind schedule if there are many candidates, and you may have to wait. Take along a book or magazine to read, or your application to review, but leave any extraneous material in the waiting room when you go in for your interview. In any event, relax and compose yourself.

The matter of dress is important. The board is forming impressions about you – from your experience, your manners, your attitude, and your appearance. Give your personal appearance careful attention. Dress your best, but not your flashiest. Choose conservative, appropriate clothing, and be sure it is immaculate. This is a business interview, and your appearance should indicate that you regard it as such. Besides, being well groomed and properly dressed will help boost your confidence.

Sooner or later, someone will call your name and escort you into the interview room. *This is it.* From here on you are on your own. It is too late for any more preparation. But remember, you asked for this opportunity to prove your fitness, and you are here because your request was granted.

What happens when you go in?

The usual sequence of events will be as follows: The clerk (who is often the board stenographer) will introduce you to the chairman of the oral board, who will introduce you to the other members of the board. Acknowledge the introductions before you sit down. Do not be surprised if you find a microphone facing you or a stenotypist sitting by. Oral interviews are usually recorded in the event of an appeal or other review.

Usually the chairman of the board will open the interview by reviewing the highlights of your education and work experience from your application – primarily for the benefit of the other members of the board, as well as to get the material into the record. Do not interrupt or comment unless there is an error or significant misinterpretation; if that is the case, do not hesitate. But do not quibble about insignificant matters. Also, he will usually ask you some question about your education, experience or your present job – partly to get you to start talking and to establish the interviewing "rapport." He may start the actual questioning, or turn it over to one of the other members. Frequently, each member undertakes the questioning on a particular area, one in which he is perhaps most competent, so you can expect each member to participate in the examination. Because time is limited, you may also expect some rather abrupt switches in the direction the questioning takes, so do not be upset by it. Normally, a board member will not pursue a single line of questioning unless he discovers a particular strength or weakness.

After each member has participated, the chairman will usually ask whether any member has any further questions, then will ask you if you have anything you wish to add. Unless you are expecting this question, it may floor you. Worse, it may start you off on an extended, extemporaneous speech. The board is not usually seeking more information. The question is principally to offer you a last opportunity to present further qualifications or to indicate that you have nothing to add. So, if you feel that a significant qualification or characteristic has been overlooked, it is proper to point it out in a sentence or so. Do not compliment the board on the thoroughness of their examination – they have been sketchy, and you know it. If you wish, merely say, "No thank you, I have nothing further to add." This is a point where you can "talk yourself out" of a good impression or fail to present an important bit of information. Remember, *you close the interview yourself.*

The chairman will then say, "That is all, Mr. _____, thank you." Do not be startled; the interview is over, and quicker than you think. Thank him, gather your belongings and take your leave. Save your sigh of relief for the other side of the door.

How to put your best foot forward

Throughout this entire process, you may feel that the board individually and collectively is trying to pierce your defenses, seek out your hidden weaknesses and embarrass and confuse you. Actually, this is not true. They are obliged to make an appraisal of your qualifications for the job you are seeking, and they want to see you in your best light. Remember, they must interview all candidates and a non-cooperative candidate may become a failure in spite of their best efforts to bring out his qualifications. Here are 15 suggestions that will help you:

1) Be natural – Keep your attitude confident, not cocky

If you are not confident that you can do the job, do not expect the board to be. Do not apologize for your weaknesses, try to bring out your strong points. The board is interested in a positive, not negative, presentation. Cockiness will antagonize any board member and make him wonder if you are covering up a weakness by a false show of strength.

2) Get comfortable, but don't lounge or sprawl

Sit erectly but not stiffly. A careless posture may lead the board to conclude that you are careless in other things, or at least that you are not impressed by the importance of the occasion. Either conclusion is natural, even if incorrect. Do not fuss with your clothing, a pencil or an ashtray. Your hands may occasionally be useful to emphasize a point; do not let them become a point of distraction.

3) Do not wisecrack or make small talk

This is a serious situation, and your attitude should show that you consider it as such. Further, the time of the board is limited – they do not want to waste it, and neither should you.

4) Do not exaggerate your experience or abilities
In the first place, from information in the application or other interviews and sources, the board may know more about you than you think. Secondly, you probably will not get away with it. An experienced board is rather adept at spotting such a situation, so do not take the chance.

5) If you know a board member, do not make a point of it, yet do not hide it
Certainly you are not fooling him, and probably not the other members of the board. Do not try to take advantage of your acquaintanceship – it will probably do you little good.

6) Do not dominate the interview
Let the board do that. They will give you the clues – do not assume that you have to do all the talking. Realize that the board has a number of questions to ask you, and do not try to take up all the interview time by showing off your extensive knowledge of the answer to the first one.

7) Be attentive
You only have 20 minutes or so, and you should keep your attention at its sharpest throughout. When a member is addressing a problem or question to you, give him your undivided attention. Address your reply principally to him, but do not exclude the other board members.

8) Do not interrupt
A board member may be stating a problem for you to analyze. He will ask you a question when the time comes. Let him state the problem, and wait for the question.

9) Make sure you understand the question
Do not try to answer until you are sure what the question is. If it is not clear, restate it in your own words or ask the board member to clarify it for you. However, do not haggle about minor elements.

10) Reply promptly but not hastily
A common entry on oral board rating sheets is "candidate responded readily," or "candidate hesitated in replies." Respond as promptly and quickly as you can, but do not jump to a hasty, ill-considered answer.

11) Do not be peremptory in your answers
A brief answer is proper – but do not fire your answer back. That is a losing game from your point of view. The board member can probably ask questions much faster than you can answer them.

12) Do not try to create the answer you think the board member wants
He is interested in what kind of mind you have and how it works – not in playing games. Furthermore, he can usually spot this practice and will actually grade you down on it.

13) Do not switch sides in your reply merely to agree with a board member
Frequently, a member will take a contrary position merely to draw you out and to see if you are willing and able to defend your point of view. Do not start a debate, yet do not surrender a good position. If a position is worth taking, it is worth defending.

14) Do not be afraid to admit an error in judgment if you are shown to be wrong

The board knows that you are forced to reply without any opportunity for careful consideration. Your answer may be demonstrably wrong. If so, admit it and get on with the interview.

15) Do not dwell at length on your present job

The opening question may relate to your present assignment. Answer the question but do not go into an extended discussion. You are being examined for a *new* job, not your present one. As a matter of fact, try to phrase ALL your answers in terms of the job for which you are being examined.

Basis of Rating

Probably you will forget most of these "do's" and "don'ts" when you walk into the oral interview room. Even remembering them all will not ensure you a passing grade. Perhaps you did not have the qualifications in the first place. But remembering them will help you to put your best foot forward, without treading on the toes of the board members.

Rumor and popular opinion to the contrary notwithstanding, an oral board wants you to make the best appearance possible. They know you are under pressure – but they also want to see how you respond to it as a guide to what your reaction would be under the pressures of the job you seek. They will be influenced by the degree of poise you display, the personal traits you show and the manner in which you respond.

ABOUT THIS BOOK

This book contains tests divided into Examination Sections. Go through each test, answering every question in the margin. We have also attached a sample answer sheet at the back of the book that can be removed and used. At the end of each test look at the answer key and check your answers. On the ones you got wrong, look at the right answer choice and learn. Do not fill in the answers first. Do not memorize the questions and answers, but understand the answer and principles involved. On your test, the questions will likely be different from the samples. Questions are changed and new ones added. If you understand these past questions you should have success with any changes that arise. Tests may consist of several types of questions. We have additional books on each subject should more study be advisable or necessary for you. Finally, the more you study, the better prepared you will be. This book is intended to be the last thing you study before you walk into the examination room. Prior study of relevant texts is also recommended. NLC publishes some of these in our Fundamental Series. Knowledge and good sense are important factors in passing your exam. Good luck also helps. So now study this Passbook, absorb the material contained within and take that knowledge into the examination. Then do your best to pass that exam.

EXAMINATION SECTION

EXAMINATION SECTION
TEST 1

DIRECTIONS: Each question or incomplete statement is followed by several suggested answers or completions. Select the one that BEST answers the question or completes the statement. *PRINT THE LETTER OF THE CORRECT ANSWER IN THE SPACE AT THE RIGHT.*

Questions 1-10.

DIRECTIONS: Questions 1 through 10 consist of four names each. In the space at the right, print the letter of the name which should be filed FIRST according to generally accepted alphabetic filing rules.

1. A. George St. John B. Thomas Santos 1.____
   C. Frances Starks D. Mary S. Stranum

2. A. Franklin Carrol B. Timothy Carrol 2.____
   C. Timothy S. Carol D. Timothy S. Carol

3. A. Christie-Barry Storage 3.____
   B. John Christie-Barry
   C. The Christie-Barry Company
   D. Anne Christie-Barrie

4. A. Inter State Travel Co. B. Interstate Car Rental 4.____
   C. Inter State Trucking D. Interstate Lending Inst.

5. A. The Los Angeles Tile Co. 5.____
   B. Anita F. Los
   C. The Lost & Found Detective Agency
   D. Jason Los-Brio

6. A. Prince Charles B. Prince Charles Coiffures 6.____
   C. Chas. F. Prince D. Thomas A. Charles

7. A. U.S. Dept. of Agriculture B. United States Aircraft Co. 7.____
   C. U.S. Air Transport, Inc. D. The United Union

8. A. Meyer's Art Shop B. Frank B. Meyer 8.____
   C. Meyers' Paint Store D. Meyer and Goldberg

9. A. David Des Laurier B. Des Moines Flower Shop 9.____
   C. Henry Desanto D. Mary L. Desta

10. A. Jeffrey Van Der Meer B. Jeffrey M. Vander 10.____
    C. Jeffrey Van D. Wallace Meer

Questions 11-20.

DIRECTIONS: Questions 11 through 20 are to be answered on the basis of the following instructions: For each such numbered set of names, addresses, and numbers listed in Columns I and II, select your answer from the following options:

A. The names in Columns I and II are different.
B. The addresses in Columns I and II are different.
C. The numbers in Columns I and II are different.
D. The names, addresses, and numbers in Columns I and II are identical.

COLUMN I   COLUMN II

11. Francis Jones
    62 Stately Avenue
    96-12446

    Francis Jones
    62 Stately Avenue
    96-21446

    11.___

12. Julio Montez
    19 Ponderosa Road
    56-73161

    Julio Montez
    19 Ponderosa Road
    56-71361

    12.___

13. Mary Mitchell
    2314 Melbourne Drive
    68-92172

    Mary Mitchell
    2314 Melbourne Drive
    68-92172

    13.___

14. Harry Patterson
    25 Dunne Street
    14-33430

    Harry Patterson
    25 Dunne Street
    14-34330

    14.___

15. Patrick Murphy
    171 West Hosmer Street
    93-81214

    Patrick Murphy
    171 West Hosmer Street
    93-18214

    15.___

16. August Schultz
    816 St. Clair Avenue
    53-40149

    August Schultz
    816 St. Claire Avenue
    53-40149

    16.___

17. George Taft
    72 Runnymede Street
    47-04033

    George Taft
    72 Runnymede Street
    47-04023

    17.___

18. Angus Henderson
    1418 Madison Street
    81-76375

    Angus Henderson
    1418 Madison Street
    81-76375

    18.___

19. Carolyn Mazur
    12 Riverview Road
    38-99615

    Carolyn Mazur
    12 Rivervane Road
    38-99615

    19.___

20. Adele Russell
    1725 Lansing Lane
    72-91962

    Adela Russell
    1725 Lansing Lane
    72-91962

    20.___

21. The reason why the analysis of mortality statistics is an IMPORTANT tool of modern public health administration is that it

    A. provides a measure of the state of health of the people of the city
    B. provides for personal records of births and deaths
    C. indicates need for methods of disposition of human remains
    D. provides a method of uncovering changes in birth or death certificates

21.____

22. When a fetal death occurs in a hospital, it should be reported to the Health Department PRIMARILY by the

    A. person in charge at the hospital
    B. attending nurse
    C. person in charge of the maternity clinic with which the attending physician or midwife is associated
    D. chief medical examiner

22.____

23. When a nurse midwife attends at or after a fetal death in a location other than a hospital, she SHOULD

    A. sign the certificate of fetal death after it has been prepared by the physician, and forward it
    B. prepare the certificate of fetal death and confidential medical report and have it examined and countersigned by a physician before forwarding it
    C. prepare the certificate of fetal death and forward it thereafter to the nearest hospital
    D. prepare the certificate of fetal death and forward it thereafter to the commissioner of health

23.____

24. According to the Health Code, which of the following next-of-kin should be notified of an adult death FIRST?

    A. Parents of deceased
    B. Spouse of deceased
    C. Children of deceased who are over 21
    D. Attorney of record

24.____

25. A registry of deaths shall be maintained and permanently preserved in each hospital. When a death occurs in a hospital, the person RESPONSIBLE for entering the death in the registry shall be

    A. the floor nursing supervisor
    B. the medical superintendent on duty
    C. any licensed physician
    D. the person who prepares the death certificate

25.____

26. The name below that would MOST likely need to be cross-referenced in an alphabetic filing system is

    A. Dr. George G. D'Arcy
    B. Mrs. Dorothy C. Crown
    C. Mr. David E. Forbes-Watkins
    D. Prof. Harry D. Van Tassell

26.____

Questions 27-30.

DIRECTIONS: Questions 27 through 30 refer to the following Certificate of Death index number: 156-74-200863.

27. The numerical component that indicates the CITY in which death occurred is

    A. 200   B. 156   C. 863   D. 74

28. The numerical component that indicates the CASE NUMBER is

    A. 00863   B. 200863   C. 156-74   D. 74-200863

29. The numerical component that indicates the BOROUGH in which death occurred is

    A. 1   B. 2   C. 3   D. 4

30. This Certificate of Death INDEX NUMBER refers to a death that occurred in

    A. the Bronx
    B. Queens
    C. Brooklyn
    D. Staten Island

KEY (CORRECT ANSWERS)

1.	A	16.	B
2.	C	17.	C
3.	D	18.	A
4.	B	19.	B
5.	B	20.	A
6.	D	21.	A
7.	C	22.	A
8.	A	23.	B
9.	C	24.	B
10.	D	25.	D
11.	C	26.	C
12.	C	27.	B
13.	D	28.	A
14.	C	29.	B
15.	C	30.	A

EXAMINATION SECTION
TEST 1

DIRECTIONS: Each question or incomplete statement is followed by several suggested answers or completions. Select the one that BEST answers the question or completes the statement. *PRINT THE LETTER OF THE CORRECT ANSWER IN THE SPACE AT THE RIGHT.*

1. Assume that you are working in an admitting office near the main entrance of a hospital. Visitors often come into your office to ask questions about hospital procedures and your supervisor has told you to be as helpful as possible in these situations.
   If a visitor comes in and asks you some questions about hospital procedures in a loud and emotional voice, the BEST course of action for you to take would be to

   A. ask him to leave the hospital and come back when he can control himself
   B. ask him to write the questions on a sheet of paper
   C. remain calm and try to answer his questions
   D. tell him to calm down or you will not answer any questions

   1._____

2. A certain hospital office administers a community health program in which members of the public are enrolled. There has been a recent change of procedure in the program and the office expects to receive a large number of letters from those enrolled asking about the change.
   Of the following, the MOST appropriate method of answering these letters is to

   A. invite each person who sends in a letter to come to the office so that the change can be explained in a personal interview
   B. prepare a form letter which explains the change of procedure and send a copy to each person who sends in a letter
   C. stamp the notation *Procedure Changed/Please Comply* on each letter and mail it back to the sender together with a description of the change of procedure
   D. telephone each person who sends in a letter and explain the change of procedure

   2._____

3. Assume that you work in a business office of a hospital and your supervisor gives you an assignment to be completed in one week. Part of the assignment requires you to obtain information from the various departments of the hospital. All departments have cooperated in giving you the required information, except one. Despite your repeated attempts to secure the information, it is still missing the day before your assignment is scheduled for completion. Even if you received the missing information immediately, you could not complete the assignment on time.
   Of the following, the FIRST action you should take in this situation is to

   A. advise your supervisor that you were not given enough time to complete the assignment
   B. contact the department which has the information you need and tell them that their failure to cooperate has made it impossible for you to complete your assignment on time
   C. explain to your supervisor why you cannot complete the assignment on time and ask him if he wishes to receive what you will be able to finish
   D. tell your supervisor that you will try to finish the assignment whenever the information is forthcoming

   3._____

4. Suppose that you work in a hospital office and you are speaking on the telephone with another employee on hospital business. While you are speaking on the telephone, a co-worker enters the office and indicates that she would like to speak with you.
Of the following, the BEST course of action for you to take in this situation is to

   A. excuse yourself on the telephone and ask your co-worker to wait until you are finished with the call
   B. ignore your co-worker and continue your telephone conversation
   C. immediately end your telephone conversation and tell your co-worker not to interrupt you again when you are speaking on the telephone
   D. tell the employee on the telephone that you have to speak with someone else and will call back as soon as you are finished

5. Assume that you are in charge of the petty cash fund for your office. When an individual wants to be paid back for an expense, he must complete a receipt explaining the expense and sign the receipt when you give him the money. One day, a clerk in your office tells you that she has just returned after delivering a package and wants to be paid back immediately for the carfare she spent. The clerk says that she has a lot of work to do in the next few hours and will complete the receipt later in the day. The BEST course of action for you to take in this situation is to

   A. explain to her that in order to receive the money she must complete and sign the receipt
   B. give her the money and leave a note on her desk reminding her to complete and sign the receipt
   C. give her the money and leave a note for yourself to make sure that she completes and signs the receipt
   D. tell her that you will give her the money and that you will complete the receipt yourself

6. Suppose that you have recently been assigned to an office and that one of your tasks is to keep files in proper order. You observe that some of your co-workers remove folders from the files, with no indication of removal. These actions have made it difficult for you to locate the folders when you need them.
Of the following, the MOST desirable method of correcting this situation is to

   A. make photocopies of the materials in all the folders and organize a duplicate set of files so that you will always have the folders readily available
   B. make sure that there are enough out-guides available and that everyone in the office is instructed to use them whenever a folder is removed
   C. tell your co-workers that they can use the files only after they tell you what folders they are going to remove
   D. ask your co-workers to leave a note on your desk whenever anyone removes a folder from the files

7. Of the following, the LEAST desirable action to take when writing out a check to a person is to

   A. fill out the check in pencil
   B. date the check
   C. number the check
   D. write the person's full name

Questions 8-17.

DIRECTIONS: Questions 8 through 17 each show in Column I names written on four cards (lettered w, x, y, z) which have to be filed. You are to choose the option (lettered A, B, C, or D) in Column II which BEST represents the proper order of filing according to the rules and sample question given below. The cards are to filed according to the following Rules for Alphabetical Filing.

RULES FOR ALPHABETICAL FILING

1. The names of individuals are filed in strict alphabetical order, first according to the last name, then according to first name or initial, and finally according to middle name or initial. For example: George Allen precedes Edward Bell; Leonard Reston precedes Lucille Reston.

2. When last names are the same, for example, A. Green and Agnes Green, the one with the initial comes before the one with the name written out when the first initials are identical.

3. When first and last names are the same, a name without a middle initial comes before one with a middle initial. For example: Ralph Simon comes before both Ralph A. Simon and Ralph Adam Simon.

4. When first and last names are the same, a name with a middle initial comes before one with a middle name beginning with the same initial. For example: Sam P. Rogers comes before Sam Paul Rogers.

5. Prefixes such as De, O', Mac, Mc, and Van are filed as written and are treated as part of the names to which they are connected. For example: Gladys McTeaque is filed before Frances Meadows.

6. Titles and designations such as Dr., Mr., and Prof, are ignored in filing.

SAMPLE QUESTION

COLUMN I

w. Jane Earl
x. James A. Earle
y. James Earl
z. J. Earle

COLUMN II

A. w, y, z, x
B. y, w, z, x
C. x, y, w, z
D. x, w, y, z

The correct way to file the cards is:
  y. James Earl
  w. Jane Earl
  z. J. Earle
  x. James A. Earle

The correct filing order is shown by the letters y, w, z, x (in that order). Since, in Column II, B appears in front of the letters y, w, z, x (in that order), B is the correct answer to the sample question.

Now answer Questions 8 through 17 using the same procedure.

4 (#1)

		COLUMN I		COLUMN II	
8.	w.	John Smith	A.	w, x, y, z	8.___
	x.	Joan Smythe	B.	y, z, x, w	
	y.	Gerald Schmidt	C.	y, z, w, x	
	z.	Gary Schmitt	D.	z, y, w, x	
9.	w.	A. Black	A.	w, x, y, z	9.___
	x.	Alan S. Black	B.	w, y, x, z	
	y.	Allan Black	C.	w, y, z, x	
	z.	Allen A. Black	D.	x, w, y, z	
10.	w.	Samuel Haynes	A.	w, x, y, z	10.___
	x.	Sam C. Haynes	B.	x, w, z, y	
	y.	David Haynes	C.	y, z, w, x	
	z.	Dave L. Haynes	D.	z, y, x, w	
11.	w.	Lisa B. McNeil	A.	x, y, w, z	11.___
	x.	Tom MacNeal	B.	x, z, y, w	
	y.	Lisa McNeil	C.	y, w, z, x	
	z.	Lorainne McNeal	D.	z, x, y, w	
12.	w.	Larry Richardson	A.	w, y, x, z	12.___
	x.	Leroy Richards	B.	y, x, z, w	
	y.	Larry S. Richards	C.	y, z, x, w	
	z.	Leroy C. Richards	D.	x, w, z, y	
13.	w.	Arlene Lane	A.	w, z, y, x	13.___
	x.	Arlene Cora Lane	B.	w, z, x, y	
	y.	Arlene Clair Lane	C.	y, x, z, w	
	z.	Arlene C. Lane	D.	z, y, w, x	
14.	w.	Betty Fish	A.	w, x, z, y	14.___
	x.	Prof. Ann Fish	B.	x, w, y, z	
	y.	Norma Fisch	C.	y, z, x, w	
	z.	Dr. Richard Fisch	D.	z, y, w, x	
15.	w.	Dr. Anthony David Lukak	A.	w, y, z, x	15.___
	x.	Mr. Steven Charles Lucas	B.	x, z, w, y	
	y.	Mr. Anthony J. Lukak	C.	z, x, y, w	
	z.	Prof. Steven C. Lucas	D.	z, x, w, y	
16.	w.	Martha Y. Lind	A.	w, y, z, x	16.___
	x.	Mary Beth Linden	B.	w, y, x, z	
	y.	Martha W. Lind	C.	y, w, z, x	
	z.	Mary Bertha Linden	D.	y, w, x, z	
17.	w.	Prof. Harry Michael MacPhelps	A.	w, z, x, y	17.___
	x.	Mr. Horace M. MacPherson	B.	w, y, z, x	
	y.	Mr. Harold M. McPhelps	C.	z, x, w, y	
	z.	Prof. Henry Martin MacPherson	D.	x, z, y, w	

18. Assume that one of your duties is to make sure that the office supply cabinet contains sufficient quantities of the forms used in your office.
Of the following, the BEST course of action for you to adopt in order to be able to perform this duty is to

    A. ask your supervisor each day whether the office is low on any form and plan to order only those forms which are mentioned
    B. decide what kind of duplicating equipment will be needed to produce copies of the forms when the current supply is exhausted
    C. plan for your office's needs and order copies of the forms before the number of copies in the cabinet falls below a minimum amount
    D. wait until one of your co-workers tells you that the office is running short of a form and then obtain copies of it as quickly as possible

19. The type of file in which reports are found under the heading *New York State-Queens* is MOST likely to be a _____ file.

    A. chronological   B. geographic
    C. numeric   D. tickler

20. Assume that you are working in the personnel office of a hospital. One day, you answer a telephone call and the caller asks to speak to one of your co-workers, Ms. Wilson, who is on sick leave. You explain this to the caller who then tells you that she is a friend of Ms. Wilson's and would like to invite her to a party but has lost Ms. Wilson's home address and telephone number. The caller then asks you if you can give her this information.
Of the following, the BEST course of action for you to take then is to

    A. give the caller the information and then leave Ms. Wilson a message about the telephone call
    B. decline to give the caller the information and ask the caller if she wants to leave a message for Ms. Wilson
    C. tell the caller that all information about hospital employees is confidential and that you cannot spend any more time on a personal telephone call
    D. tell the caller that you need some time to look up the information and ask her to call back later in the day

KEY (CORRECT ANSWERS)

1. C
2. B
3. C
4. A
5. A

6. B
7. A
8. C
9. A
10. D

11. B
12. B
13. A
14. C
15. D

16. C
17. A
18. C
19. B
20. B

TEST 2

DIRECTIONS: Each question or incomplete statement is followed by several suggested answers or completions. Select the one that BEST answers the question or completes the statement. *PRINT THE LETTER OF THE CORRECT ANSWER IN THE SPACE AT THE RIGHT.*

1. Suppose that you answer a telephone call and a woman asks to speak with your supervisor. Your supervisor, however, is speaking with someone on another telephone line. 1.____
Of the following, the BEST course of action for you to take in this situation is to

    A. ask the caller for her name and telephone number and tell her that your supervisor will return the call as soon as possible
    B. ask the caller to call again later in the day because your supervisor is busy right now
    C. explain to the caller why your supervisor cannot answer the call and ask her to wait until your supervisor can speak with her
    D. tell the caller that your supervisor is speaking on another line and ask her if she wants to wait until that call is finished or wants to leave a message

2. One morning, you receive a telephone call and the caller requests an appointment with your supervisor. Your supervisor is out of the office for the day. You tell the caller that she can meet with your supervisor at 10 A.M. the next day and she agrees. After ending this telephone conversation, you discover that your supervisor already has scheduled an appointment with someone else for that time. 2.____
Of the following, the BEST course of action for you to take in this situation is to

    A. contact your supervisor and find out which appointment he would rather keep
    B. decide which appointment is less important and cancel it
    C. try to change the appointment you made for the caller to another time
    D. wait until the next day and then tell your supervisor that he has a choice of two appointments scheduled at 10 A.M.

3. Assume that your supervisor has asked you to go to the stockroom to pick up supplies that your office has ordered. Of the following, the FIRST action you should take when you are given the supplies is to 3.____

    A. bring the supplies back to your office immediately
    B. call your supervisor to find out whether any other supplies are needed
    C. check to see whether you have received everything that was ordered
    D. sign a receipt for the supplies

Questions 4-8.

DIRECTIONS: In each of Questions 4 through 8, there is a sentence containing one underlined word. Choose the word (lettered A, B, C, or D) which means MOST NEARLY the same as the underlined word as it is used in the sentence.

4. The number of applicants exceeded the <u>anticipated</u> figure. 4.____

    A. expected   B. required   C. revised   D. necessary

5. The clerk was told to <u>collate</u> the pages of the report. 5.____

    A. destroy   B. edit   C. correct   D. assemble

6. Mr. Wells is not <u>authorized</u> to release the information.

   A. inclined   B. pleased   C. permitted   D. trained

7. The secretary chose an <u>appropriate</u> office for the meeting.

   A. empty   B. decorated   C. nearby   D. suitable

8. The employee performs a <u>complex</u> set of tasks each day.

   A. difficult   B. important   C. pleasant   D. large

9. Of the following, the MOST important purpose of a filing system generally is to
   A. reduce the number of records which must be readily available
   B. make it possible to locate information quickly
   C. organize material under the fewest number of headings
   D. provide a secure storage place if an unexpected emergency occurs

10. Assume that you answer a telephone call and the caller wishes to speak to one of your co-workers, who is out of the office.
    Of the following, the LEAST appropriate information for you to indicate on a message which you leave for your co-worker is
    A. the caller's telephone number and extension
    B. the date and time the call was received
    C. the office telephone on which the call was received
    D. your name or initials

11. The notation *cc: Mr. Rogers* appearing at the bottom of a letter is MOST likely to indicate that Mr. Rogers
    A. typed the letter
    B. is the subject of the letter
    C. wrote the rough draft of the letter for his supervisor
    D. is to receive a copy of the letter

Questions 12-16.

DIRECTIONS: Questions 12 through 16 are to be answered ONLY on the basis of the information provided in the following passage.

For some office workers, it is useful to be familiar with the four main classes of domestic mail; for others, it is essential. Each class has a different rate of postage and some have requirements concerning wrapping, sealing or special information to be placed on the package. First class mail, the class which may not be opened for postal inspection, includes letters, postcards, business reply cards, and other kinds of written matter. There are different rates for some of the kinds of cards which can be sent by first class mail. The maximum weight for an item sent by first class mail is 70 pounds. An item which is not letter size should be marked *First Class* on all sides.

Although office workers most often come into contact with first class mail, they may find it helpful to know something about the other classes. Second class mail is generally used for mailing newspapers and magazines. Publishers of these articles must meet certain U.S. Postal Service requirements in order to obtain a permit to use second class mailing rates. Third class mail, which must weigh less than 1 pound, includes printed materials and merchandise parcels. There are two rate structures for this class, a single piece rate and a bulk rate. Fourth class mail, also known as parcel post, includes packages weighing from one to 40 pounds. For more information about these classes of mail and the actual mailing rates, contact your local post office.

12. According to this passage, first class mail is the only class which

    A. has a limit on the maximum weight of an item
    B. has different rates for items within the class
    C. may not be opened for postal inspection
    D. should be used by office workers

13. According to this passage, the one of the following items which may correctly be sent by fourth class mail is a

    A. magazine weighing one-half pound
    B. package weighing one-half pound
    C. package weighing two pounds
    D. postcard

14. According to this passage, there are different postage rates for

    A. a newspaper sent by second class mail and a magazine sent by second class mail
    B. each of the classes of mail
    C. each pound of fourth class mail
    D. printed material sent by third class mail and merchandise parcels sent by third class mail

15. In order to send a newspaper by second class mail, a publisher must

    A. have met certain postal requirements and obtained a permit
    B. indicate whether he wants to use the single piece or the bulk rate
    C. make certain that the newspaper weighs less than one pound
    D. mark the newspaper *Second Class* on the top and bottom of the wrapper

16. Of the following types of information, the one which is NOT mentioned in the passage is the

    A. class of mail to which parcel post belongs
    B. kinds of items which can be sent by each class of mail
    C. maximum weight for an item sent by fourth class mail
    D. postage rate for each of the four classes of mail

17. Assume that one of your tasks is to complete a form indicating which laboratory test a doctor is ordering.
    A doctor has written an order for a laboratory test, but his writing is illegible, and you cannot tell which of two tests he is ordering.
    Of the following, the BEST course of action for you to take in this situation is to

A. show the doctor his written order, ask the doctor which test he meant to order, and then fill out the form
B. indicate both tests on the form so that you will be certain that the correct test is performed
C. send the doctor's written order to the laboratory without indicating on the form which test is to be done, since the laboratory technician will know from experience which test the doctor meant to order
D. wait for the doctor to reorder the test when he finds out that it has not been done

18. Suppose that one of your tasks is to mail an application form and covering letter to each applicant for a program administered by your office.
Of the following, the MOST appropriate notation to use at the bottom of the letter to indicate that the form is included in the envelope is

   A. Enc.   B. etc.   C. P.S.   D. R.S.V.P.

19. Of the following, the LEAST appropriate practice involved in the proper use of a file cabinet and its contents is to

   A. close a cabinet drawer immediately after using it
   B. place active files in top drawers and less active files in bottom drawers
   C. remove a file folder by holding the side of the folder, not the tab
   D. store office supplies behind files in unfilled cabinet drawers

20. Assume that you are sending out a business letter and have to write *Attention: Mrs. Williams* on the envelope. Of the following, the PROPER place on the envelope for you to write this notation is the _____ of the envelope.

   A. upper right corner of the back
   B. upper right corner on the front
   C. lower left corner of the back
   D. lower left corner on the front

KEY (CORRECT ANSWERS)

1.	D	11.	D
2.	C	12.	C
3.	C	13.	C
4.	A	14.	B
5.	D	15.	A
6.	C	16.	D
7.	D	17.	A
8.	A	18.	A
9.	B	19.	D
10.	C	20.	D

TEST 3

DIRECTIONS: Each question or incomplete statement is followed by several suggested answers or completions. Select the one that BEST answers the question or completes the statement. *PRINT THE LETTER OF THE CORRECT ANSWER IN THE SPACE AT THE RIGHT.*

1. Which of the following is the MOST efficient method of reproducing 50 copies of a single-page form letter?

    A. Carbon copying
    B. Scanning and re-editing
    C. Word processing
    D. Photocopying

2. Removing inactive documents from the active files and transferring them to a records storage center is important for which of the following reasons?

    A. The active records can be filed and retrieved more quickly.
    B. The inactive files will no longer be needed.
    C. No control is necessary with respect to the inactive files.
    D. It allows you to know which documents must be filed and which need not be filed.

3. You are trying to obtain information from someone who is to be admitted to a hospital. The person tells you in an angry tone of voice that he will not give you a certain item of information. You need this information to complete the admission form.
    Of the following, the FIRST action which you should take in this situation is to

    A. tell him that he will not be admitted unless he gives you the information
    B. tell him to wait while you go asks your supervisor to get the information from the person
    C. leave out that item of information but clearly show your anger so he will not act that way again
    D. tell him the reason why you need that item of information

4. Assume that you work in a hospital office which often receives telephone calls from people requesting information about patients in the hospital. One day, you receive a telephone call from a person who says that he is the brother of a patient. The caller asks you what is wrong with the patient and how long he will remain in the hospital.
    Of the following, the BEST course of action for you to take in this situation is to

    A. check the patient's hospital records to make sure the patient has a brother and then give the caller the information he requested
    B. contact the patient's doctor to get the information and then give it to the caller
    C. inform the caller that you are not permitted to give out that information and refer him to the patient's doctor
    D. tell the caller that you will have to check the hospital records to get the information and ask the caller for his telephone number so that you can call him back

Questions 5-14.

DIRECTIONS: Questions 5 through 14 are based on the following table, which shows the number of persons admitted to and discharged from each of five hospitals for each of the first six months of 2005. Admissions are shown under the columns labeled *ADM* and discharges under the columns labeled *DIS*.

ADMISSIONS AND DISCHARGES
January-June, 2005

MONTH	HOSPITAL L		HOSPITAL M		HOSPITAL N		HOSPITAL O		HOSPITAL P	
	ADM	DIS	ADM	DIS	ADM	DIS	ADM	DIS	ADM	DIS
JAN.	367	291	389	372	738	694	1101	942	1567	1373
FEB.	447	473	411	376	874	841	1353	1296	1754	1687
MAR.	426	437	403	436	831	813	1297	1358	1690	1740
APR.	403	390	370	385	794	850	1057	1190	1389	1650
MAY	370	411	361	390	680	692	984	1039	1195	1210
JUNE	334	355	377	384	630	619	1121	1043	1125	1065

5. The TOTAL number of admissions to the five hospitals for the month of April was

   A. 3,833   B. 3,952   C. 3,983   D. 4,013

6. The TOTAL number of discharges from Hospital N for the months of April, May, and June was

   A. 1,159   B. 2,104   C. 2,161   D. 2,251

7. The TOTAL number of admissions to Hospitals L, M, and O for the month of February was

   A. 1,732   B. 2,101   C. 2,145   D. 2,211

8. The TOTAL number of discharges from the five hospitals for the month of January was

   A. 3,542   B. 3,672   C. 3,832   D. 4,162

9. For which month were there MORE discharges at each of the five hospitals than there were admissions?

   A. January   B. March   C. May   D. June

10. The average number of admissions each month at Hospital O for the first six months of 2005 was MOST NEARLY

    A. 1,097   B. 1,152   C. 1,163   D. 1,196

11. Of the total number of admissions at the five hospitals for the month of March, what percentage, to the nearest whole percent, was admitted to Hospital P?

    A. 29%   B. 32%   C. 34%   D. 36%

12. The average number of discharges from each of the five hospitals for the month of May was MOST NEARLY

    A. 748   B. 754   C. 762   D. 764

13. Of the total number of admissions to the five hospitals for the month of June, what percentage, to the nearest whole percent, was admitted to Hospital M?

    A. 7%   B. 9%   C. 11%   D. 13%

14. On the basis of the information given in the table, which one of the following statements is CORRECT?
The number of

    A. admissions to each hospital for the month of April was less than the number of admissions for the month of March
    B. admissions to Hospital L increased each month from January through April and decreased each month from May through June
    C. discharges from each hospital for the month of June was less than the number of discharges for the month of May
    D. discharges from Hospital O increased each month from January through March and decreased each month from April through June

Questions 15-20.

DIRECTIONS: Questions 15 through 20 consist of three lines of code letters and numbers. The numbers on each line should correspond with the code letters on the same line in accordance with the table below.

Code Letter	F	X	L	M	R	W	T	S	B	H
Corresponding Number	0	1	2	3	4	5	6	7	8	9

On some of the lines, an error exists in the coding. Compare the letters and numbers in each question carefully. If you find an error or errors on
    only one of the lines in the question, mark your answer A;
    any two lines in the question, mark your answer B;
    all three lines in the question, mark your answer C;
    none of the lines in the question, mark your answer D.

SAMPLE QUESTION: LTSXHMF   2671930
                             TBRWHLM   6845913
                             SXLBFMR   5128034

In the above sample, the first line is correct since each code letter listed has the correct corresponding number. On the second line, an error exists because code letter L should have the number 2 instead of the number 1. On the third line, an error exists because the code letter S should have the number 7 instead of the number 5. Since there are errors on two of the three lines, the correct answer is B.

15. XMWBHLR   1358924
    FWSLRHX   0572491
    MTXBLTS   3618267

16. XTLSMRF   1627340
    BMHRFLT   8394026
    HLTSWRX   9267451

4 (#3)

17. LMBSFXS   2387016   17.____
    RWLHBSX   4532871
    SMFXBHW   7301894

18. RSTWTSML   47657632   18.____
    LXRMHFBS   21439087
    FTLBMRWX   06273451

19. XSRSBWFM   17478603   19.____
    BRMXRMXT   84314216
    XSTFBWRL   17609542

20. TMSBXHLS   63781927   20.____
    RBSFLFWM   48702053
    MHFXWTRS   39015647

KEY (CORRECT ANSWERS)

1.	D	11.	D
2.	A	12.	A
3.	D	13.	C
4.	C	14.	A
5.	D	15.	D
6.	C	16.	A
7.	D	17.	C
8.	B	18.	B
9.	C	19.	C
10.	B	20.	D

EXAMINATION SECTION
TEST 1

DIRECTIONS: Each question or incomplete statement is followed by several suggested answers or completions. Select the one that BEST answers the question or completes the statement. *PRINT THE LETTER OF THE CORRECT ANSWER IN THE SPACE AT THE RIGHT.*

1. In filing records by subject, you should be MOST concerned with the 1.____

   A. name of the sender
   B. main topic of the letter
   C. date of the correspondence
   D. alphabetic cross reference

2. When arranging the medical record cards of patients in alphabetical order, the one of the following which should be filed THIRD is 2.____

   A. Charles A. Clarke B. James Clark
   C. Joan Carney D. Mae Cohen

3. The one of the following names which should be filed FIRST is 3.____

   A. Benjamin Dermody B. Frank Davidson
   C. Matthew Davids D. Seymour Diana

4. Vital statistics include data relating to 4.____

   A. births, deaths, and marriages
   B. the cost of food, clothing, and shelter
   C. the number of children per family unit
   D. diseases and their comparative mortality rates

Questions 5-10.

DIRECTIONS: Questions 5 through 10 are to be answered on the basis of the usual rules for alphabetical filing. For each question, indicate in the space at the right the letter preceding the name which should be filed THIRD in alphabetical order.

5. A. Hesselberg, Norman J. B. Hesselman, Nathan B. 5.____
   C. Hazel, Robert S. D. Heintz, August J.

6. A. Oshins, Jerome B. O'Shaugn, F.J. 6.____
   C. O'Shaugn, F.J. D. O'Shea, Frances

7. A. Petrie, Joshua A. B. Pendleton, Oscar 7.____
   C. Pertwee, Joshua D. Perkins, Warren G.

8. A. Morganstern, Alfred B. Morganstern, Albert 8.____
   C. Monroe, Mildred D. Modesti, Ernest

9. A. More, Stewart B. Moorhead, Jay 9.____
   C. Moore, Benjamin D. Moffat, Edith

10. A. Ramirez, Paul   B. Revere, Pauline   10.____
    C. Ramos, Felix   D. Ramazotti, Angelo

Questions 11-20.

DIRECTIONS: Questions 11 through 20 are to be answered on the basis of the usual rules of filing. Column I lists, next to the numbers 11 to 20, the names of 10 clinic patients. Column II lists, next to the letters A to D, the headings of file drawers into which you are to place the medical records of these patients. For each question, indicate in the space at the right the letter preceding the heading of the file drawer in which the record should be filed.

COLUMN I   COLUMN II

11. Charles Coughlin   A. Cab-Cep   11.____
12. Mary Carstairs   B. Ceq-Cho   12.____
13. Joseph Collin   C. Chr-Coj   13.____
14. Thomas Chelsey   D. Cok-Czy   14.____
15. Cedric Chalmers   15.____
16. Mae Clarke   16.____
17. Dora Copperhead   17.____
18. Arnold Cohn   18.____
19. Charlotte Crumboldt   19.____
20. Frances Celine   20.____

Questions 21-25.

DIRECTIONS: Questions 21 through 25 are to be answered on the basis of the chart below.

ATTENDANCE OF PATIENTS AT Y HEALTH CENTER
FOR WEEK OF APRIL 10

CLINIC	NUMBER SUMMONED FOR				NUMBER REPORTED TO			
	BABY	CHEST	EYE	V.D.	BABY	CHEST	EYE	V.D.
Monday	30	42	36	38	29	40	33	35
Tuesday	33	29	34	37	30	29	31	36
Wednesday	38	31	45	42	35	30	40	40
Thursday	41	48	41	32	36	45	39	28
Friday	35	37	39	36	33	35	37	32

21. On the basis of the above chart, it is CORRECT to say that _____ Clinic during the week.   21._____

    A. more patients were summoned to the Baby Clinic than to the Chest
    B. the same number of patients were absent from the Eye Clinic and the Baby
    C. more patients reported to the Eye Clinic than to the Chest
    D. more patients were summoned to the V.D. Clinic than to the Eye

22. On the basis of the above chart, the daily average number of patients summoned to the Eye Clinic exceeds the daily average reporting to the Eye Clinic by   22._____

    A. 3   B. 7   C. 11   D. 15

23. The percentage of all patients summoned to Y Health Center on Thursday who failed to report for their appointments is   23._____

    A. less than 5%
    B. more than 5% but less than 10%
    C. more than 10% but less than 15%
    D. more than 15%

24. The number of patients summoned for the entire week to the Eye Clinic exceeds the number of patients summoned to the Baby Clinic by   24._____

    A. 6   B. 9   C. 13   D. 18

25. The total number of patients who reported to Y Health Center for the week is   25._____

    A. 683   B. 693   C. 724   D. 744

KEY (CORRECT ANSWERS)

1. B	11. D
2. A	12. A
3. C	13. D
4. A	14. B
5. A	15. B
6. D	16. C
7. C	17. D
8. B	18. C
9. B	19. D
10. C	20. A

21. C
22. A
23. B
24. D
25. B

TEST 2

DIRECTIONS: Each question or incomplete statement is followed by several suggested answers or completions. Select the one that BEST answers the question or completes the statement. *PRINT THE LETTER OF THE CORRECT ANSWER IN THE SPACE AT THE RIGHT.*

Questions 1-8.

DIRECTIONS: Questions 1 through 8 are to be answered on the basis of the usual rules of filing. Column I lists, next to the numbers 1 to 8, the names of 8 clinic patients. Column II lists, next to the letters A to O, the headings of file drawers into which you are to place the records of these patients. In the space at the right, corresponding to each name listed in Column I, print the letter preceding the heading of the file drawer in which the record should be filed.

COLUMN I		COLUMN II	
1.	Thomas Adams	A.	Aab-Abi
2.	Joseph Albert	B.	Abj-Ach
3.	Frank Anaster	C.	Aci-Aco
4.	Charles Abt	D.	Acp-Ada
5.	John Alfred	E.	Adb-Afr
6.	Louis Aron	F.	Afs-Ago
7.	Francis Amos	G.	Agp-Ahz
8.	William Adler	H.	Aia-Ako
		I.	Akp-Ald
		J.	Ale-Amo
		K.	Amp-Aor
		L.	Aos-Apr
		M.	Aps-Asi
		N.	Asj-Ati
		O.	Atj-Awz

1.___
2.___
3.___
4.___
5.___
6.___
7.___
8.___

Questions 9-14.

DIRECTIONS: In answering Questions 9 through 14, alphabetize the four names listed in each question; then print in the corresponding space at the right the letter of the answer containing the four numbers preceding the alphabetized names to show the CORRECT alphabetical arrangement of the four names.

9. 1. Frank Adam   2. Frank Aarons
    3. Frank Aaron   4. Frank Adams
    The CORRECT answer is:

    A. 2, 3, 1, 4   B. 4, 2, 1, 3
    C. 1, 2, 4, 3   D. 3, 2, 1, 4

10. 1. Richard Lavine   2. Richard Levine
    3. Edward Lawrence   4. Edward Loraine
    The CORRECT answer is:

    A. 1, 2, 3, 4   B. 3, 1, 2, 4
    C. 1, 3, 2, 4   D. 2, 4, 3, 1

11. 1. G. Frank Adam   2. Frank Adam
    3. Fanny Adam   4. Franklin Adam
    The CORRECT answer is:

    A. 3, 4, 1, 2   B. 2, 1, 3, 4
    C. 3, 2, 4, 1   D. 2, 3, 4, 1

12. 1. George Cohn   2. Richard Cohen
    3. Thomas Cohane   4. George Cohan
    The CORRECT answer is:

    A. 2, 1, 3, 4   B. 4, 1, 3, 2
    C. 3, 1, 4, 2   D. 4, 3, 2, 1

13. 1. Paul Shultz   2. Robert Schmid
    3. Joseph Schwartz   4. Edward Schmidt
    The CORRECT answer is:

    A. 2, 4, 3, 1   B. 2, 1, 3, 4
    C. 3, 4, 1, 2   D. 1, 2, 4, 3

14. 1. Peter Consilazio   2. Frank Consolezio
    3. Robert Consalizio   4. Ella Consolizio
    The CORRECT answer is:

    A. 3, 4, 1, 2   B. 3, 1, 2, 4
    C. 1, 2, 4, 3   D. 3, 2, 1, 4

Questions 15-25.

DIRECTIONS: For Questions 15 through 25, select the letter preceding the word which means MOST NEARLY the same as the word in capitals.

15. LEGIBLE

    A. readable   B. eligible   C. learned   D. lawful

16. OBSERVE

    A. assist   B. watch   C. correct   D. oppose

17. HABITUAL

    A. punctual   B. occasional
    C. usual   D. actual

18. CHRONOLOGICAL

    A. successive
    B. earlier
    C. later
    D. studious

19. ARREST

    A. punish
    B. run
    C. threaten
    D. stop

20. ABSTAIN

    A. refrain
    B. indulge
    C. discolor
    D. spoil

21. TOXIC

    A. poisonous
    B. decaying
    C. taxing
    D. defective

22. TOLERATE

    A. fear
    B. forgive
    C. allow
    D. despise

23. VENTILATE

    A. vacate
    B. air
    C. extricate
    D. heat

24. SUPERIOR

    A. perfect
    B. subordinate
    C. lower
    D. higher

25. EXTREMITY

    A. extent
    B. limb
    C. illness
    D. execution

KEY (CORRECT ANSWERS)

1. D	11. C
2. I	12. D
3. K	13. A
4. B	14. B
5. J	15. A
6. M	16. B
7. J	17. C
8. E	18. A
9. D	19. D
10. C	20. A

21. A
22. C
23. B
24. D
25. B

TEST 3

DIRECTIONS: Each question or incomplete statement is followed by several suggested answers or completions. Select the one that BEST answers the question or completes the statement. *PRINT THE LETTER OF THE CORRECT ANSWER IN THE SPACE AT THE RIGHT.*

Questions 1-20.

DIRECTIONS: Column I below lists words used in medical practice. Column II lists phrases which describe the words in Column I. In the space at the right, opposite the number preceding each of the words in Column I, place the letter preceding the phrase in Column II which BEST describes the word in Column I.

COLUMN I

1. Abrasion
2. Aseptic
3. Cardiac
4. Catarrh
5. Contamination
6. Dermatology
7. Disinfectant
8. Dyspepsia
9. Epidemic
10. Epidermis
11. Incubation
12. Microscope
13. Pediatrics
14. Plasma
15. Prenatal
16. Retina
17. Syphilis
18. Syringe
19. Toxemia
20. Vaccine

COLUMN II

A. A disturbance of digestion
B. Destroying the germs of disease
C. A general poisoning of the blood
D. An instrument used for injecting fluids
E. A scraping off of the skin
F. Free from disease germs
G. An apparatus for viewing internal organs by means of x-rays
H. An instrument for assisting the eye in observing minute objects
I. An inoculable immunizing agent
J. The extensive prevalence in a community of a disease
K. Chemical product of an organ
L. Preceding birth
M. Fever
N. Branch of medical science that relates to skin and its diseases
O. Fluid part of the blood
P. The science of hygienic care of children
Q. Infection by contact
R. Relating to the heart
S. Inner structure of the eye
T. Outer portion of the skin
U. Pertaining to the ductless glands
V. An infectious venereal disease
X. The development of an infectious disease from the period of infection to that of the appearance of the first symptoms
Y. Simple inflammation of a mucous membrane
Z. An instrument for measuring blood pressure

1. _____
2. _____
3. _____
4. _____
5. _____
6. _____
7. _____
8. _____
9. _____
10. _____
11. _____
12. _____
13. _____
14. _____
15. _____
16. _____
17. _____
18. _____
19. _____
20. _____

21. The fluoroscope is used CHIEFLY to

   A. provide a permanent picture of the condition of internal organs at a given time
   B. make a chart of the action of the muscles of the heart
   C. observe the internal structure and functioning of the organs of the body at a given time
   D. produce heat in the tissues of the body

22. A stethoscope is an instrument used for

   A. determining the blood pressure
   B. taking the body temperature
   C. chest examinations
   D. determining the amount of sugar in the blood

23. The Dick test is used to determine susceptibility to

   A. measles
   B. scarlet fever
   C. diphtheria
   D. chicken pox

24. The aorta is a(n)

   A. bone   B. artery   C. ligament   D. nerve

25. The esophagus is part of the

   A. alimentary canal
   B. abdominal wall
   C. mucous membrane
   D. circulatory system

KEY (CORRECT ANSWERS)

1.	E	11.	X
2.	F	12.	H
3.	R	13.	P
4.	Y	14.	O
5.	Q	15.	L
6.	N	16.	S
7.	B	17.	V
8.	A	18.	D
9.	J	19.	C
10.	T	20.	I

21. C
22. C
23. B
24. B
25. A

EXAMINATION SECTION
TEST 1

DIRECTIONS: Each question or incomplete statement is followed by several suggested answers or completions. Select the one that BEST answers the question or completes the statement. *PRINT THE LETTER OF THE CORRECT ANSWER IN THE SPACE AT THE RIGHT.*

Questions 1-15.

DIRECTIONS: In the following questions numbered 1 through 15, the word in capitals is the name of an anatomical part which is a segment of a larger structure or system. For each question, select the letter preceding the structure or system of which the word in capitals is a part.

1. ESOPHAGUS

    A. circulatory system
    C. submaxillary
    B. bronchi
    D. respiratory system

2. ALVEOLI

    A. nervous system
    C. endocrine system
    B. lungs
    D. muscle

3. DELTOID

    A. upper arm
    C. circulatory system
    B. rib cage
    D. superior vena cava

4. FEMORAL ARTERY

    A. right ventricle
    C. circulatory system
    B. left auricle
    D. lymphatic system

5. BRACKIAL PLEXUS

    A. circulatory system
    C. respiratory system
    B. nervous system
    D. bronchi

6. ERYTHROCYTE

    A. lymph glands
    C. blood
    B. skeletal system
    D. large intestine

7. STERNUM

    A. spinal column
    C. nervous system
    B. muscular system
    D. skeletal system

8. THYMUS

    A. endocrine system
    C. parathyroids
    B. pituitary gland
    D. adrenals

9. MANDIBLE

    A. pelvis   B. head   C. liver   D. stomach

10. PECTORAL

    A. skeletal system   B. patella
    C. chest   D. digestive tract

11. CORNEA

    A. arm   B. eye   C. blood   D. lymph

12. CRANIUM

    A. circulatory system   B. left auricle
    C. skeletal system   D. abdomen

13. TRAPEZIUS

    A. breastbone   B. muscular system
    C. endocrine system   D. spinal column

14. MEGALOBLAST

    A. blood   B. pelvis   C. spleen   D. head

15. ADRENAL

    A. mouth   B. respiratory system
    C. liver   D. endocrine system

Questions 16-25.

DIRECTIONS: The following questions numbered 16 through 25 are concerned with various categories of diseases. For each question, select the letter preceding the disease or condition which MOST properly belongs to the category listed.

16. BONE DISEASE

    A. arrhythmia   B. arthritis
    C. edema   D. gastritis

17. DISEASE OF THE DIGESTIVE SYSTEM

    A. diabetes   B. osteomyelitis
    C. ileitis   D. conjunctivitis

18. DISEASE OF THE RESPIRATORY SYSTEM

    A. cyanosis   B. poliomyelitis
    C. jaundice   D. bronchiectasis

19. DISEASE OF THE HEART

    A. hepatitis   B. influenza
    C. encephalitis   D. myocarditis

20. DISEASE OF THE BLOOD

    A. leukemia   B. diphtheria
    C. pneumonia   D. colitis

21. NUTRITIONAL DISEASE   21.____

   A. hyperemia   B. mononucleosis
   C. trichinosis   D. scurvy

22. DISEASE OF THE NERVOUS SYSTEM   22.____

   A. amebiasis   B. parkinsonism
   C. ascariasis   D. tapeworm

23. PARASITIC DISEASE   23.____

   A. salmonella   B. neuralgia
   C. hemophilia   D. bursitis

24. SKIN DISEASE   24.____

   A. hydrocephalus   B. leprosy
   C. adenitis   D. angina

25. DISEASE OF THE URINARY TRACT   25.____

   A. myasthenia gravis   B. colitis
   C. hydronephrosis   D. dermatitis

KEY (CORRECT ANSWERS)

1.	D	11.	B
2.	B	12.	C
3.	A	13.	B
4.	C	14.	A
5.	B	15.	D
6.	C	16.	B
7.	D	17.	C
8.	A	18.	D
9.	B	19.	D
10.	C	20.	A

21. D
22. B
23. A
24. B
25. C

TEST 2

DIRECTIONS: Each question or incomplete statement is followed by several suggested answers or completions. Select the one that BEST answers the question or completes the statement. *PRINT THE LETTER OF THE CORRECT ANSWER IN THE SPACE AT THE RIGHT.*

Questions 1-10.

DIRECTIONS: Questions 1 through 10 are concerned with various categories of diseases. For each question, select the letter preceding the disease or condition which MOST properly belongs to the category listed.

1. DISEASE OF THE HEART 1.____
   - A. diabetes
   - B. tachycardia
   - C. osteoporosis
   - D. adenitis

2. SKIN DISEASE 2.____
   - A. cholelithiasis
   - B. colitis
   - C. psoriasis
   - D. encephalitis

3. DISEASE OF THE BLOOD 3.____
   - A. polycythemia
   - B. ileitis
   - C. psoitis
   - D. dermatitis

4. DISEASE OF THE RESPIRATORY SYSTEM 4.____
   - A. dysentery
   - B. angina
   - C. hemophilia
   - D. pneumonia

5. DISEASE OF THE DIGESTIVE SYSTEM 5.____
   - A. periastitis
   - B. bronchiectasis
   - C. enteritis
   - D. pertussis

6. PARASITIC DISEASE 6.____
   - A. ascariasis
   - B. nephritis
   - C. hyperemia
   - D. neuralgia

7. NUTRITIONAL DISEASE 7.____
   - A. entasis
   - B. pellagra
   - C. amebiasis
   - D. diphtheria

8. BONE DISEASE 8.____
   - A. gangrene
   - B. epilepsy
   - C. osteochondritis
   - D. bronchitis

9. DISEASE OF THE NERVOUS SYSTEM 9.____
   - A. mononucleosis
   - B. gallstones
   - C. jaundice
   - D. multiple sclerosis

10. DISEASE OF THE URINARY TRACT 10.____
    A. hydrocephalus B. glomerulonephritis
    C. cyanosis   D. bursitis

Questions 11-25.

DIRECTIONS: For the following questions 11 through 25, select the letter preceding the part or system of the body which is CHIEFLY affected by the disease in capitals.

11. CONJUNCTIVITIS 11.____
    A. ear   B. intestines
    C. eye   D. liver

12. EMPHYSEMA 12.____
    A. heart   B. bronchial tubes
    C. pancreas D. lymph nodes

13. CHOLELITHIASIS 13.____
    A. muscles B. liver
    C. bones   D. common bile duct

14. PYELONEPHRITIS 14.____
    A. intestinal tract B. arterial walls
    C. ligaments   D. urinary tract

15. EPILEPSY 15.____
    A. nervous system B. pancreas
    C. thyroid   D. stomach

16. DYSENTERY 16.____
    A. tendons   B. kidneys
    C. intestines D. brain

17. ERYTHROBLASTOSIS 17.____
    A. kidneys   B. blood
    C. endocrine system D. large intestine

18. GLAUCOMA 18.____
    A. blood vessels B. cortex
    C. cerebellum   D. eye

19. OSTEOPOROSIS 19.____
    A. bones   B. central nervous system
    C. adrenals D. lymph nodes

20. MENINGITIS 20.____
    A. nasal passages B. intestinal tract
    C. spinal cord   D. urinary tract

21. BURSITIS

    A. urinary tract   B. bones
    C. nasal passages   D. heart

22. ENDOCARDITIS

    A. cortex   B. kidneys   C. pancreas   D. heart

23. DIVERTICULOSIS

    A. thyroid   B. endocrine system
    C. intestinal tract   D. kidneys

24. ENCEPHALITIS

    A. brain   B. vessels   C. kidneys   D. eye

25. ILEITIS

    A. nervous system   B. blood
    C. liver   D. intestinal tract

KEY (CORRECT ANSWERS)

1.	B	11.	C
2.	C	12.	B
3.	A	13.	D
4.	D	14.	D
5.	C	15.	A
6.	A	16.	C
7.	B	17.	B
8.	C	18.	D
9.	D	19.	A
10.	B	20.	C

21. B
22. D
23. C
24. A
25. D

EXAMINATION SECTION
TEST 1

DIRECTIONS: Each question or incomplete statement is followed by several suggested answers or completions. Select the one that BEST answers the question or completes the statement. *PRINT THE LETTER OF THE CORRECT ANSWER IN THE SPACE AT THE RIGHT.*

Questions 1-20.

DIRECTIONS: Column I below lists words used in medical practice. Column II lists phrases which describe the words in Column I. Opposite the number preceding each of the words in Column I, place the letter preceding the phrase in Column II which BEST describes the word in Column I.

COLUMN I

1. Abrasion
2. Aseptic
3. Cardiac
4. Catarrh
5. Contamination
6. Dermatology
7. Disinfectant
8. Dyspepsia
9. Epidemic
10. Epidermis
11. Incubation
12. Microscope
13. Pediatrics
14. Plasma
15. Prenatal
16. Retina
17. Syphilis
18. Syringe
19. Toxemia
20. Vaccine

COLUMN II

A. A disturbance of digestion
B. Destroying the germs of disease
C. A general poisoning of the blood
D. An instrument used for injecting fluids
E. A scraping off of the skin
F. Free from disease germs
G. An apparatus for viewing internal organs by means of x-rays
H. An instrument for assisting the eye in observing minute objects
I. An inoculable immunizing agent
J. The extensive prevalence in a community of a
K. Chemical product of an organ
L. Preceding birth
M. Fever
N. The branch of medical science that relates to the skin and its diseases
O. Fluid part of the blood
P. The science of the hygienic care of children
Q. Infection by contact
R. Relating to the heart
S. Inner structure of the eye
T. Outer portion of the skin
U. Pertaining to the ductless glands
V. An infectious venereal disease
W. The development of an infectious disease from the period of infection to that of the appearance of the first symptoms
X. Simple inflammation of a mucous membrane
Y. An instrument for measuring blood pressure

Questions 21-25.

DIRECTIONS: Each of Questions 21 through 25 consists of four words. Three of these words belong together. One word does NOT belong with the other three. For each group of words, you are to select the one word which does NOT belong with the other three words.

21. A. conclude   B. terminate   C. initiate   D. end   21.___

22. A. deficient   B. inadequate   22.___
    C. excessive   D. insufficient

23. A. rare   B. unique   C. unusual   D. frequent   23.___

24. A. unquestionable   B. uncertain   24.___
    C. doubtful   D. indefinite

25. A. stretch   B. contract   C. extend   D. expand   25.___

KEY (CORRECT ANSWERS)

1. E
2. F
3. R
4. X
5. Q

6. N
7. B
8. A
9. J
10. T

11. W
12. H
13. P
14. O
15. L

16. S
17. V
18. D
19. C
20. I

21. C
22. C
23. D
24. A
25. B

TEST 2

DIRECTIONS: Each question or incomplete statement is followed by several suggested answers or completions. Select the one that BEST answers the question or completes the statement. *PRINT THE LETTER OF THE CORRECT ANSWER IN THE SPACE AT THE RIGHT.*

Questions 1-4.

DIRECTIONS: Questions 1 through 4 pertain to the meaning of terms which may be encountered in laboratory work. For each question, select the option whose meaning is MOST NEARLY the same as that of the numbered item.

1. Atrophied 1.____
   - A. enlarged
   - B. relaxed
   - C. strengthened
   - D. wasted

2. Leucocyte 2.____
   - A. white cell
   - B. red cell
   - C. epithelial cell
   - D. dermal cell

3. Permeable 3.____
   - A. volatile
   - B. variable
   - C. flexible
   - D. penetrable

4. Attenuate 4.____
   - A. dilute
   - B. infect
   - C. oxidize
   - D. strengthen

Questions 5-11.

DIRECTIONS: For Questions 5 through 11, select the letter preceding the word which means MOST NEARLY the same as the first word.

5. legible 5.____
   - A. readable   B. eligible   C. learned   D. lawful

6. observe 6.____
   - A. assist   B. watch   C. correct   D. oppose

7. habitual 7.____
   - A. punctual
   - B. occasional
   - C. usual
   - D. actual

8. chronological 8.____
   - A. successive
   - B. earlier
   - C. later
   - D. studious

9. arrest
   A. punish   B. run   C. threaten   D. stop

10. abstain
    A. refrain   B. indulge   C. discolor   D. spoil

11. toxic
    A. poisonous   B. decaying
    C. taxing   D. defective

12. The *initial* contact is of great importance in setting a pattern for future relations.
    The word *initial*, as used in this sentence, means MOST NEARLY
    A. first   B. written   C. direct   D. hidden

13. The doctor prescribed a diet which was *adequate* for the patient's needs.
    The word *adequate*, as used in this sentence, means MOST NEARLY
    A. insufficient   B. unusual
    C. required   D. enough

14. The child was reported to be suffering from a vitamin *deficiency*.
    The word *deficiency*, as used in this sentence, means MOST NEARLY
    A. surplus   B. infection   C. shortage   D. injury

15. In obtaining medical case data, a medical record librarian should discourage the patient from giving *irrelevant* information.
    The word *irrelevant*, as used in this sentence, means MOST NEARLY
    A. too detailed   B. pertaining to relatives
    C. insufficient   D. inappropriate

16. The doctor requested that a *tentative* appointment be made for the patient.
    The word *tentative*, as used in this sentence, means MOST NEARLY
    A. definite   B. subject to change
    C. later   D. of short duration

17. The black plague resulted in an usually high *mortality rate* in the population of Europe.
    The term *mortality rate*, as used in this sentence, means MOST NEARLY
    A. future immunity of the people
    B. death rate
    C. general weakening of the health of the people
    D. sickness rate

18. The public health assistant was asked to file a number of *identical* reports on the case.
    The word *identical*, as used in this sentence, means MOST NEARLY
    A. accurate   B. detailed   C. same   D. different

19. The nurse assisted in *the biopsy* of the patient.
    The word *biopsy*, as used in this sentence, means MOST NEARLY

    A. autopsy
    B. excision and diagnostic study of tissue
    C. biography and health history
    D. administering of anesthesia

20. The assistant noted that the swelling on the patient's face had *subsided*.
    The word *subsided*, as used in this sentence, means MOST NEARLY

    A. become aggravated   B. increased
    C. vanished   D. abated

21. The patient was given food *intravenously*.
    The word *intravenously*, as used in this sentence, means MOST NEARLY

    A. orally   B. against his will
    C. through the veins   D. without condiment

Questions 22-25.

DIRECTIONS: Each of Questions 22 through 25 consists of four words. Three of these words belong together. One word does NOT belong with the other three. For each group of words, you are to select the one word which does NOT belong with the other three words.

22. A. accelerate   B. quicken   C. accept   D. hasten
23. A. sever   B. rupture   C. rectify   D. tear
24. A. innocuous   B. injurious C. dangerous   D. harmful
25. A. adulterate   B. contaminate
    C. taint   D. disinfect

KEY (CORRECT ANSWERS)

1. D	11. A	21. C
2. A	12. A	22. C
3. D	13. D	23. C
4. A	14. C	24. A
5. A	15. D	25. D
6. B	16. B	
7. C	17. B	
8. A	18. C	
9. D	19. B	
10. A	20. D	

TEST 3

DIRECTIONS: Each question or incomplete statement is followed by several suggested answers or completions. Select the one that BEST answers the question or completes the statement. *PRINT THE LETTER OF THE CORRECT ANSWER IN THE SPACE AT THE RIGHT.*

Questions 1-25.

DIRECTIONS: Each of Questions 1 through 25 consists of a word, in capitals, followed by four suggested meanings of the word. For each question, indicate in the space at the right the letter preceding the word which means MOST NEARLY the same as the word in capitals.

1. TEMPORARY

    A. permanently
    C. at the same time
    B. for a limited time
    D. frequently

2. INQUIRE

    A. order   B. agree   C. ask   D. discharge

3. SUFFICIENT

    A. enough
    C. thorough
    B. inadequate
    D. capable

4. AMBULATORY

    A. bedridden
    C. walking
    B. left-handed
    D. laboratory

5. DILATE

    A. enlarge   B. contract   C. revise   D. restrict

6. NUTRITIOUS

    A. protective
    C. fattening
    B. healthful
    D. nourishing

7. CONGENITAL

    A. with pleasure
    C. likeable
    B. defective
    D. existing from birth

8. ISOLATION

    A. sanitation
    C. rudeness
    B. quarantine
    D. exposure

9. SPASM

    A. splash   B. twitch   C. space   D. blow

1.____
2.____
3.____
4.____
5.____
6.____
7.____
8.____
9.____

38

10. HEMORRHAGE
    A. bleeding
    B. ulcer
    C. hereditary disease
    D. lack of blood

10.____

11. NOXIOUS
    A. gaseous B. harmful C. soothing D. repulsive

11.____

12. PYOGENIC
    A. disease producing
    B. fever producing
    C. pus forming
    D. water forming

12.____

13. RENAL
    A. brain B. heart C. kidney D. stomach

13.____

14. ENDEMIC
    A. epidemic
    B. endermic
    C. endoblast
    D. peculiar to a particular people or locality, as a disease

14.____

15. MACULATION
    A. reticulation
    B. inoculation
    C. maturation
    D. defilement

15.____

16. TOLERATE
    A. fear B. forgive C. allow D. despise

16.____

17. VENTILATE
    A. vacate B. air C. extricate D. heat

17.____

18. SUPERIOR
    A. perfect
    B. subordinate
    C. lower
    D. higher

18.____

19. EXTREMITY
    A. extent B. limb C. illness D. execution

19.____

20. DIVULGED
    A. unrefined B. secreted C. revealed D. divided

20.____

21. SIPHON
    A. drain B. drink C. compute D. discard

21.____

22. EXPIRATION
    A. trip
    B. demonstration
    C. examination
    D. end

22.____

23. AEROSOL
    A. a gas dispersed in a liquid
    B. a liquid dispersed in a gas
    C. a liquid dispersed in a solid
    D. a solid dispersed in a liquid

24. ETIOLOGY
    A. cause of a disease
    B. method of cure
    C. method of diagnosis
    D. study of insects

25. IN VITRO
    A. in alkali
    B. in the body
    C. in the test tube
    D. in vacuum

KEY (CORRECT ANSWERS)

1. B
2. C
3. A
4. C
5. A

6. D
7. D
8. B
9. B
10. A

11. B
12. C
13. C
14. D
15. D

16. C
17. B
18. D
19. B
20. C

21. A
22. D
23. B
24. A
25. C

RECORD KEEPING
EXAMINATION SECTION
TEST 1

DIRECTIONS: Each question or incomplete statement is followed by several suggested answers or completions. Select the one that BEST answers the question or completes the statement. *PRINT THE LETTER OF THE CORRECT ANSWER IN THE SPACE AT THE RIGHT.*

Questions 1-15.

DIRECTIONS: Questions 1 through 15 are to be answered on the basis of the following list of company names below. Arrange a file alphabetically, word-by-word, disregarding punctuation, conjunctions, and apostrophes. Then answer the questions.

> A Bee C Reading Materials
> ABCO Parts
> A Better Course for Test Preparation
> AAA Auto Parts Co.
> A-Z Auto Parts, Inc.
> Aabar Books
> Abbey, Joanne
> Boman-Sylvan Law Firm
> BMW Autowerks
> C Q Service Company
> Chappell-Murray, Inc.
> E&E Life Insurance
> Emcrisco
> Gigi Arts
> Gordon, Jon & Associates
> SOS Plumbing
> Schmidt, J.B. Co.

1. Which of these files should appear FIRST?   1.____
   A. ABCO Parts
   B. A Bee C Reading Materials
   C. A Better Course for Test Preparation
   D. AAA Auto Parts Co.

2. Which of these files should appear SECOND?   2.____
   A. A-Z Auto Parts, Inc.
   B. A Bee C Reading Materials
   C. A Better Course for Test Preparation
   D. AAA Auto Parts Co.

41

2 (#1)

3. Which of these files should appear THIRD? 3.____
   A. ABCO Parts   B. A Bee C Reading Materials
   C. Aabar Books   D. AAA Auto Parts Co.

4. Which of these files should appear FOURTH? 4.____
   A. Aabar Books   B. ABCO Parts
   C. Abbey, Joanne   D. AAA Auto Parts Co.

5. Which of these files should appear LAST? 5.____
   A. Gordon, Jon & Associates B. Gigi Arts
   C. Schmidt, J.B. Co.   D. SOS Plumbing

6. Which of these files should appear between A-Z Auto Parts, Inc. and Abbey, Joanne? 6.____
   A. A Bee C Reading Materials
   B. AAA Auto Parts Co.
   C. ABCO Parts
   D. A Better Course for Test Preparation

7. Which of these files should appear between ABCO Parts and Aabar Books? 7.____
   A. A Bee C Reading Materials B. Abbey, Joanne
   C. Aabar Books   D. A-Z Auto Parts

8. Which of these files should appear between Abbey, Joanne and Boman-Sylvan Law Firm? 8.____
   A. A Better Course for Test Preparation
   B. BMW Autowerks
   C. Chappell-Murray, Inc.
   D. Aabar Books

9. Which of these files should appear between Abbey, Joanne and C Q Service? 9.____
   A. A-Z Auto Parts, Inc.   B. BMW Autowerks
   C. Choices A and B   D. Chappell-Murray, Inc.

10. Which of these files should appear between C Q Service Company and Emcrisco? 10.____
    A. Chappell-Murray, Inc.   B. E&E Life Insurance
    C. Gigi Arts   D. Choices A and B

11. Which of these files should NOT appear between C Q Service Company and E&E Life Insurance? 11.____
    A. Gordon, Jon & Associates B. Emcrisco
    C. Gigi Arts   D. All of the above

12. Which of these files should appear between Chappell-Murray, Inc. and Gigi Arts?
    A. C Q Service Inc., E&E Life Insurance, and Emcrisco
    B. Emcrisco, E&E Life Insurance, and Gordon, Jon & Associates
    C. E&E Life Insurance, and Emcrisco
    D. Emcrisco and Gordon, Jon & Associates

13. Which of these files should appear between Gordon, Jon & Associates and SOS Plumbing?
    A. Gigi Arts
    B. Schmidt, J.B. Co.
    C. Choices A and B
    D. None of the above

14. Each of the choices lists the four files in their proper alphabetical order EXCEPT
    A. E&E Life Insurance; Gigi Arts; Gordon, Jon & Associates; SOS Plumbing
    B. E&E Life Insurance; Emcrisco; Gigi Arts; SOS Plumbing
    C. Emcrisco; Gordon, Jon & Associates; SOS Plumbing; Schmidt, J.B. Co.
    D. Emcrisco; Gigi Arts; Gordon, Jon & Associates; SOS Plumbing

15. Which of the choices lists the four files in their proper alphabetical order?
    A. Gigi Arts; Gordon, Jon & Associates; SOS Plumbing; Schmidt, J.B. Co.
    B. Gordon, Jon & Associates; Gigi Arts; Schmidt, J.B. Co.; SOS Plumbing
    C. Gordon, Jon & Associates; Gigi Arts; SOS Plumbing; Schmidt, J.B. Co.
    D. Gigi Arts; Gordon, Jon & Associates; Schmidt, J.B. Co.; SOS Plumbing

16. The alphabetical filing order of two businesses with identical names is determined by the
    A. length of time each business has been operating
    B. addresses of the businesses
    C. last name of the company president
    D. no one of the above

17. In an alphabetical filing system, if a business name includes a number, it should be
    A. disregarded
    B. considered a number and placed at the end of an alphabetical section
    C. treated as though it were written in words and alphabetized accordingly
    D. considered a number and placed at the beginning of an alphabetical section

18. If a business name includes a contraction (such as *don't* or *it's*), how should that word be treated in an alphabetical system?
    A. Divide the word into its separate parts and treat it as two words
    B. Ignore the letters that come after the apostrophe
    C. Ignore the word that contains the contraction
    D. Ignore the apostrophe and consider all letters in the contraction

19. In what order should the parts of an address be considered when using an   19._____
    alphabetical filing system?
    A. City or town; state; street name; house or building number
    B. State; city or town; street name; house or building number
    C. House or building number; street name; city or town; state
    D. Street name; city or town; state

20. A business record should be cross-referenced when a(n)   20._____
    A. organization is known by an abbreviated name
    B. business has a name change because of a sale, incorporation, or other reason
    C. business is known by a *coined* or common name which differs from a dictionary spelling
    D. all of the above

21. A geographical filing system is MOST effective when   21._____
    A. location is more important than name
    B. many names or titles sound alike
    C. dealing with companies who have offices all over the world
    D. filing personal and business files

Questions 22-25.

DIRECTIONS: Questions 22 through 25 are to be answered on the basis of the list of items below, which are to be filed geographically. Organize the items geographically and then answer the questions.

   I. University Press at Berkeley, U.S.
  II. Maria Sanchez, Mexico City, Mexico
 III. Great Expectations Ltd. in London, England
  IV. Justice League, Cape Town, South Africa, Africa
   V. Crown Pearls Ltd. in London, England
  VI. Joseph Prasad in London, England

22. Which of the following arrangements of the items is composed according to the   22._____
    policy of: *Continent, Country, City, Firm or Individual Name*?
    A. V, III, IV, VI, II, I   B. IV, V, III, VI, II, I
    C. I, IV, V, III, VI, II   D. IV, V, III, VI, I, II

23. Which of the following files is arranged according to the policy of: 23._____
    Continent, Country, City, Firm or Individual Name?
    A. South Africa; Africa; Cape Town; Justice League
    B. Mexico; Mexico City; Maria Sanchez
    C. North America; United States; Berkeley; University Press
    D. England; Europe; London; Prasad, Joseph

5 (#1)

24. Which of the following arrangements of the items is composed according to the policy of: *Country, City, Firm or Individual Name*?   24.____
    A. V, VI, III, II, IV, I
    B. I, V, VI, III, II, IV
    C. VI, V, III, II, IV, I
    D. V, III, VI, II, IV, I

25. Which of the following files is arranged according to a policy of: *Country, City, Firm or Individual Name*?   25.____
    A. England; London; Crown Pearls Ltd.
    B. North America; United States; Berkeley; University Press
    C. Africa; Cape Town; Justice League
    D. Mexico City; Mexico; Maria Sanchez

26. Under which of the following circumstances would a phonetic filing system be MOST effective?   26.____
    A. When the person in charge of filing can't spell very well
    B. With large files with names that sound alike
    C. With large files with names that are spelled alike
    D. All of the above

Questions 27-29.

DIRECTIONS: Questions 27 through 29 are to be answered on the basis of the following list of numerical files.

    I. 391-023-100
    II. 361-132-170
    III. 385-732-200
    IV. 381-432-150
    V. 391-632-387
    VI. 361-423-303
    VII. 391-123-271

27. Which of the following arrangements of the files follows a consecutive-digit system?   27.____
    A. II, III, IV, I
    B. I, V, VII, III
    C. II, IV, III, I
    D. III, I, V, VII

28. Which of the following arrangements follows a terminal-digit system?   28.____
    A. I, VII, II, IV, III
    B. II, I, IV, V, VII
    C. VII, VI, V, IV, III
    D. I, IV, II, III, VII

29. Which of the following lists follows a middle-digit system?   29.____
    A. I, VII, II, VI, IV, V, III
    B. I, II, VII, IV, VI, V, III
    C. VII, II, I, III, V, VI, IV
    D. VII, I, II, IV, VI, V, III

Questions 30-31.

DIRECTIONS: Questions 30 and 31 are to be answered on the basis of the following information.

    I. Reconfirm Laura Bates appointment with James Caldecort on December 12 at 9:30 A.M.
    II. Laurence Kinder contact Julia Lucas on August 3 and set up a meeting for week of September 23 at 4 P.M.
    III. John Lutz contact Larry Waverly on August 3 and set up appointment for September 23 at 9:30 A.M.
    IV. Call for tickets for Gerry Stanton August 21 for New Jersey on September 23, flight 143 at 4:43 P.M.

30. A chronological file for the above information would be
    A. IV, III, II, I   B. III, II, IV, I   C. IV, II, III, I   D. III, I, II, IV

31. Using the above information, a chronological file for the date September 23 would be
    A. II, III, IV   B. III, I, IV   C. III, II, IV   D. IV, III, II

Questions 32-34.

DIRECTIONS: Questions 32 through 34 are to be answered on the basis of the following information.

    I. Call Roger Epstein, Ashoke Naipaul, Jon Anderson, and Sara Washingon on April 19 at 1:00 P.M. to set up meeting with Alika D'Ornay for June 6 in New York.
    II. Call Martin Ames before noon on April 19 to confirm afternoon meeting with Bob Greenwood on April 20th.
    III. Set up meeting room at noon for 2:30 P.M. meeting on April 19th.
    IV. Ashley Stanton contact Bob Greenwood at 9:00 A.M. on April 20 and set up meeting for June 6 at 8:30 A.M.
    V. Carol Guiland contact Shelby Van Ness during afternoon of April 20 and set up meeting for June 6 at 10:00 A.M.
    VI. Call airline and reserve tickets on June 6 for Roger Epstein trip to Denver on July 8.
    VII. Meeting at 2:30 P.M. on April 19th.

32. A chronological file for all of the above information would be
    A. II, I, III, VII, V, IV, VI   B. III, VII, II, I, IV, V, VI
    C. III, VII, I, II, V, IV, VI   D. II, III, I, VII, IV, V, VI

33. A chronological file for the date of April 19th would be
    A. II, III, VII, I   B. II, III, I, VII   C. VII, I, III, II   D. III, VII, I, II

34. Add the following information to the file, and then create a chronological file   34._____
    for April 20th: VIII. April 20: 3:00 P.M. meeting between Bob Greenwood and
    Martin Ames.
    A. IV, V, VIII   B. IV, VIII, V   C. VIII, V, IV   D. V, IV, VIII

35. The PRIMARY advantage of computer records over a manual system is   35._____
    A. speed of retrieval   B. accuracy
    C. cost   D. potential file loss

KEY (CORRECT ANSWERS)

1.	B	11.	D	21.	A	31.	C
2.	C	12.	C	22.	B	32.	D
3.	D	13.	B	23.	C	33.	B
4.	A	14.	C	24.	D	34.	A
5.	D	15.	D	25.	A	35.	A
6.	C	16.	B	26.	B		
7.	B	17.	C	27.	C		
8.	B	18.	D	28.	D		
9.	C	19.	A	29.	A		
10.	D	20.	D	30.	B		

READING COMPREHENSION
UNDERSTANDING AND INTERPRETING WRITTEN MATERIAL
EXAMINATION SECTION
TEST 1

Questions 1-8.

DIRECTIONS: Each question or incomplete statement is followed by several suggested answers or completions. Select the one that BEST answers the question or completes the statement. *PRINT THE LETTER OF THE CORRECT ANSWER IN THE SPACE AT THE RIGHT.*

Questions 1 and 2.

DIRECTIONS: Your answers to Questions 1 and 2 must be based ONLY on the information given in the following paragraph.

Hospitals maintained wholly by public taxation may treat only those compensation cases which are emergencies and may not treat such emergency cases longer than the emergency exists; provided, however, that these restrictions shall not be applicable where there is not available a hospital other than a hospital maintained wholly by taxation.

1. According to the above paragraph, compensation cases

    A. are regarded as emergency cases by hospitals maintained wholly by public taxation
    B. are seldom treated by hospitals maintained wholly by public taxation
    C. are treated mainly by privately endowed hospitals
    D. may be treated by hospitals maintained wholly by public taxation if they are emergencies

2. According to the above paragraph, it is MOST reasonable to conclude that where a privately endowed hospital is available,

    A. a hospital supported wholly by public taxation may treat emergency compensation cases only so long as the emergency exists
    B. a hospital supported wholly by public taxation may treat any compensation cases
    C. a hospital supported wholly by public taxation must refer emergency compensation cases to such a hospital
    D. the restrictions regarding the treatment of compensation cases by a tax-supported hospital are not wholly applicable

Questions 3-7.

DIRECTIONS: Answer Questions 3 through 7 ONLY according to the information given in the following passage.

THE MANUFACTURE OF LAUNDRY SOAP

The manufacture of soap is not a complicated process. Soap is a fat or an oil, plus an alkali, water and salt. The alkali used in making commercial laundry soap is caustic soda. The salt used is the same as common table salt. A fat is generally an animal product that is not a liquid at room temperature. If heated, it becomes a liquid. An oil is generally liquid at room temperature. If the temperature is lowered, the oil becomes a solid just like ordinary fat.

At the soap plant, a huge tank five stories high, called a *kettle,* is first filled part way with fats and then the alkali and water are added. These ingredients are then heated and boiled together. Salt is then poured into the top of the boiling solution; and as the salt slowly sinks down through the mixture, it takes with it the glycerine which comes from the melted fats. The product which finally comes from the kettle is a clear soap which has a moisture content of about 34%. This clear soap is then chilled so that more moisture is driven out. As a result, the manufacturer finally ends up with a commercial laundry soap consisting of 88% clear soap and only 12% moisture.

3. An ingredient used in making laundry soap is

   A. table sugar
   B. potash
   C. glycerine
   D. caustic soda

4. According to the above passage, a difference between fats and oils is that fats

   A. cost more than oils
   B. are solid at room temperature
   C. have less water than oils
   D. are a liquid animal product

5. According to the above passage, the MAIN reason for using salt in the manufacture of soap is to

   A. make the ingredients boil together
   B. keep the fats in the kettle melted
   C. remove the glycerine
   D. prevent the loss of water from the soap

6. According to the passage, the purpose of chilling the clear soap is to

   A. stop the glycerine from melting
   B. separate the alkali from the fats
   C. make the oil become solid
   D. get rid of more moisture

7. According to the passage, the percentage of moisture in commercial laundry soap is

   A. 12%   B. 34%   C. 66%   D. 88%

8. The x-ray has gone into business. Developed primarily to aid in diagnosing human ills, the machine now works in packing plants, in foundries, in service stations, and in a dozen ways to contribute to precision and accuracy in industry.
The above statement means *most nearly* that the x-ray

   A. was first developed to aid business
   B. is of more help to business than it is to medicine
   C. is being used to improve the functioning of business
   D. is more accurate for packing plants than it is for foundries

8.____

Questions 9-25.

DIRECTIONS: Each question consists of a statement. You are to indicate whether the statement is TRUE (T) or FALSE (F). *PRINT THE LETTER OF THE CORRECT ANSWER IN THE SPACE AT THE RIGHT.*

Questions 9-12.

DIRECTIONS: Read the paragraph below about *shock* and then answer Questions 9 through 12 according to the information given in the paragraph.

SHOCK

While not found in all injuries, shock is present in all serious injuries caused by accidents. During shock, the normal activities of the body slow down. This partly explains why one of the signs of shock is a pale, cold skin, since insufficient blood goes to the body parts during shock.

9. If the injury caused by an accident is serious, shock is sure to be present. 9.____

10. In shock, the heart beats faster than normal. 10.____

11. The face of a person suffering from shock is usually red and flushed. 11.____

12. Not enough blood goes to different parts of the body during shock. 12.____

Questions 13-18.

DIRECTIONS: Questions 13 through 18, inclusive, are to be answered SOLELY on the basis of the information contained in the following statement and NOT upon any other information you may have.

Blood transfusions are given to patients at the hospital upon recommendation of the physicians attending such cases. The physician fills out a *Request for Blood Transfusion* form in duplicate and sends both copies to the Medical Director's office, where a list is maintained of persons called *donors* who desire to sell their blood for transfusions. A suitable donor is selected, and the transfusion is given. Donors are, in many instances, medical students and employees of the hospital. Donors receive twenty-five dollars for each transfusion.

13. According to the above paragraph, a blood donor is paid twenty-five dollars for each transfusion. 13.____

14. According to the above paragraph, only medical students and employees of the hospital are selected as blood donors.   14.___

15. According to the above paragraph, the *Request for Blood Transfusion* form is filled out by the patient and sent to the Medical Director's office.   15.___

16. According to the above paragraph, a list of blood donors is maintained in the Medical Director's office.   16.___

17. According to the above paragraph, cases for which the attending physicians recommend blood transfusions are usually emergency cases.   17.___

18. According to the above paragraph, one copy of the *Request for Blood Transfusion* form is kept by the patient and one copy is sent to the Medical Director's office.   18.___

Questions 19-25.

DIRECTIONS: Questions 19 through 25, inclusive, are to be answered SOLELY on the basis of the information contained in the following passage and NOT upon any other information you may have.

Before being admitted to a hospital ward, a patient is first interviewed by the Admitting Clerk, who records the patient's name, age, sex, race, birthplace, and mother's maiden name. This clerk takes all of the money and valuables that the patient has on his person. A list of the valuables is written on the back of the envelope in which the valuables are afterwards placed. Cash is counted and placed in a separate envelope, and the amount of money and the name of the patient are written on the outside of the envelope. Both envelopes are sealed, fastened together, and placed in a compartment of a safe.

An orderly then escorts the patient to a dressing room where the patient's clothes are removed and placed in a bundle. A tag bearing the patient's name is fastened to the bundle. A list of the contents of the bundle is written on property slips, which are made out in triplicate. The information contained on the outside of the envelopes containing the cash and valuables belonging to the patient is also copied on the property slips.

According to the above passage,

19. patients are escorted to the dressing room by the Admitting Clerk.   19.___

20. the patient's cash and valuables are placed together in one envelope.   20.___

21. the number of identical property slips that are made out when a patient is being admitted to a hospital ward is three.   21.___

22. the full names of both parents of a patient are recorded by the Admitting Clerk before a patient is admitted to a hospital ward.   22.___

23. the amount of money that a patient has on his person when admitted to the hospital is entered on the patient's property slips.   23.___

24. an orderly takes all the money and valuables that a patient has on his person.   24.___

25. the patient's name is placed on the tag that is attached to the bundle containing the patient's clothing.   25.___

KEY (CORRECT ANSWERS)

1.	D	11.	F
2.	A	12.	T
3.	D	13.	T
4.	B	14.	F
5.	C	15.	F
6.	D	16.	T
7.	A	17.	T
8.	C	18.	F
9.	T	19.	F
10.	F	20.	F

21. T
22. F
23. T
24. F
25. T

TEST 2

DIRECTIONS: Each question or incomplete statement is followed by several suggested answers or completions. Select the one that BEST answers the question or completes the statement. *PRINT THE LETTER OF THE CORRECT ANSWER IN THE SPACE AT THE RIGHT.*

Questions 1-4.

DIRECTIONS: Questions 1 through 4 are to be answered in accordance with the following paragraphs.

One fundamental difference between the United States health care system and the health care systems of some European countries is the way that hospital charges for long-term illnesses affect their citizens.

In European countries such as England, Sweden, and Germany, citizens can face, without fear, hospital charges due to prolonged illness, no matter how substantial they may be. Citizens of these nations are required to pay nothing when they are hospitalized, for they have prepaid their treatment as taxpayers when they were well and were earning incomes.

On the other hand, the United States citizen, in spite of the growth of payments by third parties which include private insurance carriers as well as public resources, has still to shoulder 40 percent of hospital care costs, while his private insurance contributes only 25 percent and public resources the remaining 35 percent.

Despite expansion of private health insurance and social legislation in the United States, out-of-pocket payments for hospital care by individuals have steadily increased. Such payments, currently totalling $23 billion, are nearly twice as high as ten years ago.

Reform is inevitable and, when it comes, will have to reconcile sharply conflicting interests. Hospital staffs are demanding higher and higher wages. Hospitals are under pressure by citizens, who as patients demand more and better services but who as taxpayers or as subscribers to hospital insurance plans, are reluctant to pay the higher cost of improved care. An acceptable reconciliation of these interests has so far eluded legislators and health administrators in the United States.

1. According to the above passage, the one of the following which is an ADVANTAGE that citizens of England, Sweden, and Germany have over United States citizens is that, when faced with long-term illness,   1.___

    A. the amount of out-of-pocket payments made by these European citizens is small when compared to out-of-pocket payments made by United States citizens
    B. European citizens have no fear of hospital costs no matter how great they may be
    C. more efficient and reliable hospitals are available to the European citizen than is available to the United States citizens
    D. a greater range of specialized hospital care is available to the European citizens than is available to the United States citizens

2. According to the above passage, reform of the United States system of health care must reconcile all of the following EXCEPT

   A. attempts by health administrators to provide improved hospital care
   B. taxpayers' reluctance to pay for the cost of more and better hospital services
   C. demands by hospital personnel for higher wages
   D. insurance subscribers' reluctance to pay the higher costs of improved hospital care

3. According to the above passage, the out-of-pocket payments for hospital care that individuals made ten years ago was APPROXIMATELY _____ billion.

   A. $32   B. $23   C. $12   D. $3

4. According to the above passage, the GREATEST share of the costs of hospital care in the United States is paid by

   A. United States citizens
   B. private insurance carriers
   C. public resources
   D. third parties

Questions 5-8.

DIRECTIONS: Questions 5 through 8 are to be answered SOLELY on the basis of the information contained in the following passage.

Effective cost controls have been difficult to establish in most hospitals in the United States. Ways must be found to operate hospitals with reasonable efficiency without sacrificing quality and in a manner that will reduce the amount of personal income now being spent on health care and the enormous drain on national resources. We must adopt a new public objective of providing higher quality health care at significantly lower cost. One step that can be taken to achieve this goal is to carefully control capital expenditures for hospital construction and expansion. Perhaps the way to start is to declare a moratorium on all hospital construction and to determine the factors that should be considered in deciding whether a hospital should be built. Such factors might include population growth, distance to the nearest hospital, availability of medical personnel, and hospital bed shortage.

A second step to achieve the new objective is to increase the ratio of out-of-hospital patient to in-hospital patient care. This can be done by using separate health care facilities other than hospitals to attract patients who have increasingly been going to hospital clinics and overcrowding them. Patients should instead identify with a separate health care facility to keep them out of hospitals.

A third step is to require better hospital operating rules and controls. This step might include the review of a doctor's performance by other doctors, outside professional evaluations of medical practice, and required refresher courses and re-examinations for doctors. Other measures might include obtaining mandatory second opinions on the need for surgery in order to avoid unnecessary surgery, and outside review of work rules and procedures to eliminate unnecessary testing of patients.

A fourth step is to halt the construction and public subsidizing of new medical schools and to fill whatever needs exist in professional coverage by emphasizing the medical training of physicians with specialities that are in short supply and by providing a better geographic distribution of physicians and surgeons.

5. According to the above passage, providing higher quality health care at lower cost can be achieved by the

   A. greater use of out-of-hospital facilities
   B. application of more effective cost controls on doctors' fees
   C. expansion of improved in-hospital patient care services at hospital clinics
   D. development of more effective training programs in hospital administration

6. According to the above passage, the one of the following which should be taken into account in determining if a hospital should be constructed is the

   A. number of out-of-hospital health care facilities
   B. availability of public funds to subsidize construction
   C. number of hospitals under construction
   D. availability of medical personnel

7. According to the above passage, it is IMPORTANT to operate hospitals efficiently because

   A. they are currently in serious financial difficulties
   B. of the need to reduce the amount of personal income going to health care
   C. the quality of health care services has deteriorated
   D. of the need to increase productivity goals to take care of the growing population in the United States

8. According to the above passage, which one of the following approaches is MOST LIKELY to result in better operating rules and controls in hospitals?

   A. Allocating doctors to health care facilities on the basis of patient population
   B. Equalizing the workloads of doctors
   C. Establishing a physician review board to evaluate the performance of other physicians
   D. Eliminating unnecessary outside review of patient testing

Questions 9-14.

DIRECTIONS: Questions 9 through 14 are to be answered SOLELY on the basis of the information contained in the following passage.

The United States today is the only major industrial nation in the world without a system of national health insurance or a national health service. Instead, we have placed our prime reliance on private enterprise and private health insurance to meet the need. Yet, in a recent year, of the 180 million Americans under 65 years of age, 34 million had no hospital insurance, 38 million had no surgical insurance, 63 million had no out-patient x-ray and laboratory insurance, 94 million had no insurance for prescription drugs, and 103 million had no insurance for physician office visits or home visits. Some 35 million Americans under the age of 65 had no health insurance whatsoever. Some 64 million additional Americans under age 65 had health insurance coverage that was less than that provided to the aged under Medicare.

Despite more than three decades of enormous growth, the private health insurance industry today pays benefits equal to only one-third of the total cost of private health care, leaving the rest to be borne by the patient—essentially the same ratio which held true a decade ago. Moreover, nearly all private health insurance is limited; it provides partial benefits, not comprehensive benefits; acute care, not preventive care; it siphons off the young and healthy, and ignores the poor and medically indigent. The typical private carrier usually pays only the cost of hospital care, forcing physicians and patients alike to resort to wasteful and inefficient use of hospital facilities, thereby giving further impetus to the already soaring costs of hospital care. Valuable hospital beds are used for routine tests and examinations. Unnecessary hospitalization, unnecessary surgery, and unnecessarily extended hospital stays are encouraged. These problems are exacerbated by the fact that administrative costs of commercial carriers are substantially higher than they are for Blue Shield, Blue Cross, or Medicare.

9. According to the above passage, the PROPORTION of total private health care costs paid by private health insurance companies today as compared to ten years ago has

    A. *increased* by approximately one-third
    B. *remained* practically the same
    C. *increased* by approximately two-thirds
    D. *decreased* by approximately one-third

10. According to the above passage, the one of the following which has contributed MOST to wasteful use of hospital facilities is the

    A. increased emphasis on preventive health care
    B. practice of private carriers of providing comprehensive health care benefits
    C. increased hospitalization of the elderly and the poor
    D. practice of a number of private carriers of paying only for hospital care costs

11. Based on the information in the above passage, which one of the following patients would be LEAST likely to receive benefits from a typical private health insurance plan? A

    A. young patient who must undergo an emergency appendectomy
    B. middle-aged patient who needs a costly series of x-ray and laboratory tests for diagnosis of gastrointestinal complaints
    C. young patient who must visit his physician weekly for treatment of a chronic skin disease
    D. middle-aged patient who requires extensive cancer surgery

12. Which one of the following is the MOST accurate inference that can be drawn from the above passage?

    A. Private health insurance has failed to fully meet the health care needs of Americans.
    B. Most Americans under age 65 have health insurance coverage better than that provided to the elderly under Medicare.
    C. Countries with a national health service are likely to provide poorer health care for their citizens than do countries that rely primarily on private health insurance.
    D. Hospital facilities in the United States are inadequate to meet the nation's health care needs.

13. Of the total number of Americans under age 65, what percentage belonged in the combined category of persons with NO health insurance or health insurance less than that provided to the aged under Medicare?

   A. 19%   B. 36%   C. 55%   D. 65%

14. According to the above passage, the one of the following types of health insurance which covered the SMALLEST number of Americans under age 65 was

   A. hospital insurance
   B. surgical insurance
   C. insurance for prescription drugs
   D. insurance for physician office or home visits

Questions 15-17.

DIRECTIONS: Questions 15 through 17 are to be answered SOLELY on the basis of the information contained in the following passage.

Statistical studies have demonstrated that disease and mortality rates are higher among the poor than among the more affluent members of our society. Periodic surveys conducted by the United States Public Health Service continue to document a higher prevalence of infectious and chronic diseases within low income families. While the basic life style and living conditions of the poor are to a considerable extent responsible for this less favorable health status, there are indications that the kind of health care received by the poor also plays a significant role. The poor are less likely to be aware of the concepts and practices of scientific medicine and less likely to seek health care when they need it. Moreover, they are discouraged from seeking adequate health care by the depersonalization, disorganization, and inadequate emphasis on preventive care which characterize the health care most often provided for them.

To achieve the objective of better health care for the poor, the following approaches have been suggested: encouraging the poor to seek preventive care as well as care for acute illness and to establish a lasting one-to-one relationship with a single physician who can treat the poor patient as a whole individual; sufficient financial subsidy to put the poor on an equal footing with *paying patients,* thereby giving them the opportunity to choose from among available health services providers; inducements to health services providers to establish public clinics in poverty areas; and legislation to provide for health education, earlier detection of disease, and coordinated health care.

15. According to the above passage, the one of the following which is a function of the United States Public Health Service is

   A. gathering data on the incidence of infectious diseases
   B. operating public health clinics in poverty areas lacking private physicians
   C. recommending legislation for the improvement of health care in the United States
   D. encouraging the poor to participate in programs aimed at the prevention of illness

16. According to the above passage, the one of the following which is MOST characteristic of the health care currently provided for the poor is that it

   A. aims at establishing clinics in poverty areas
   B. enables the poor to select the health care they want through the use of financial subsidies
   C. places insufficient stress on preventive health care
   D. over-emphasizes the establishment of a one-to-one relationship between physician and patient

17. The above passage IMPLIES that the poor lack the financial resources to

   A. obtain adequate health insurance coverage
   B. select from among existing health services
   C. participate in health education programs
   D. lobby for legislation aimed at improving their health care

Questions 18-20.

DIRECTIONS: Questions 18 through 20 are to be answered SOLELY on the basis of the information contained in the following passage.

The concept of *affiliation,* developed more than ten years ago, grew out of a series of studies which found evidence of faulty care, surgery of *questionable* value and other undesirable conditions in the city's municipal hospitals. The affiliation agreements signed shortly thereafter were designed to correct these deficiencies by assuring high quality medical care. In general, the agreements provided the staff and expertise of a voluntary hospital—sometimes connected with a medical school—to operate various services or, in some cases, all of the professional divisions of a specific municipal hospital. The municipal hospitals have paid for these services, which last year cost the city $200 million, the largest single expenditure of the Health and Hospitals Corporation. In addition, the municipal hospitals have provided to the voluntary hospitals such facilities as free space for laboratories and research. While some experts agree that affiliation has resulted in improvements in some hospital care, they contend that many conditions that affiliation was meant to correct still exist. In addition, accountability procedures between the Corporation and voluntary hospitals are said to be so inadequate that audits of affiliation contracts of the past five years revealed that there may be more than $200 million in charges for services by the voluntary hospitals which have not been fully substantiated. Consequently, the Corporation has proposed that future agreements provide accountability in terms of funds, services supplied, and use of facilities by the voluntary hospitals.

18. According to the above passage, *affiliation* may BEST be defined as an agreement whereby

   A. voluntary hospitals pay for the use of municipal hospital facilities
   B. voluntary and municipal hospitals work to eliminate duplication of services
   C. municipal hospitals pay voluntary hospitals for services performed
   D. voluntary and municipal hospitals transfer patients to take advantage of specialized services

19. According to the above passage, the MAIN purpose for setting up the *affiliation* agreement was to

    A. supplement the revenues of municipal hospitals
    B. improve the quality of medical care in municipal hospitals
    C. reduce operating costs in municipal hospitals
    D. increase the amount of space available to municipal hospitals

20. According to the above passage, inadequate accountability procedures have resulted in

    A. unsubstantiated charges for services by the voluntary hospitals
    B. emphasis on research rather than on patient care in municipal hospitals
    C. unsubstantiated charges for services by the municipal hospitals
    D. economic losses to voluntary hospitals

Questions 21-25.

DIRECTIONS: Questions 21 through 25 are to be answered SOLELY on the basis of the information contained in the following passage.

The payment for medical services covered under the Outpatient Medical Insurance Plan (OMI) may be made, by OMI, directly to a physician or to the OMI patient. If the physician and the patient agree that the physician is to receive payment directly from OMI, the payment will be officially assigned to the physician; this is the assignment method. If payment is not assigned, the patient receives payment directly from OMI based on an itemized bill he submits, regardless of whether or not he has already paid his physician.

When a physician accepts assignment of the payment for medical services, he agrees that total charges will not be more than the allowed charge determined by the OMI carrier administering the program. In such cases, the OMI patient pays any unmet part of the $85 annual deductible, plus 10 percent of the remaining charges to the physician. In unassigned claims, the patient is responsible for the total amount charged by the physician. The patient will then be reimbursed by the program 90 percent of the allowed charges in excess of the annual deductible.

The rates of acceptance of assignments provide a measure of how many OMI patients are spared *administrative participation* in the program. Because physicians are free to accept or reject assignments, the rate in which assignments are made provide a general indication of the medical community's satisfaction with the OMI program, especially with the level of amounts paid by the program for specific services and the promptness of payment.

21. According to the above passage, in order for a physician to receive payment directly from OMI for medical services to an OMI patient, the physician would have to accept the assignment of payment, to have the consent of the patient, AND to

    A. submit to OMI a paid itemized bill
    B. collect from the patient 90% of the total bill
    C. collect from the patient the total amount of the charges for his services, a portion of which he will later reimburse the patient
    D. agree that his charges for services to the patient will not exceed the amount allowed by the program

22. According to the above passage, if a physician accepts assignment of payment, the patient pays

   A. the total amount charged by the physician and is reimbursed by the program for 90 percent of the allowed charges in excess of the applicable deductible
   B. any unmet part of the $85 annual deductible, plus 90 percent of the remaining charges
   C. the total amount charged by the physician and is reimbursed by the program for 10 percent of the allowed charges in excess of the $85 annual deductible
   D. any unmet part of the $85 annual deductible, plus 10 percent of the remaining charges

23. A physician has accepted the assignment of payment for charges to an OMI patient. The physician's charges, all of which are allowed under OMI, amount to $115. This is the first time the patient has been eligible for OMI benefits and the first time the patient has received services from this physician.
   According to the above passage, the patient must pay the physician

   A. $27   B. $76.50   C. $88   D. $103.50

24. In an unassigned claim, a physician's charges, all of which are allowed under OMI, amount to $165. The patient paid the physician the full amount of the bill.
   If this is the FIRST time the patient has been eligible for OMI benefits, he will receive from OMI a reimbursement of

   A. $72   B. $80   C. $85   D. $93

25. According to the above passage, if the rate of acceptance of assignments by physicians is high, it is LEAST appropriate to conclude that the medical community is generally satisfied with the

   A. supplementary medical insurance program
   B. levels of amounts paid to physicians by the program
   C. number of OMI patients being spared administrative participation in the program
   D. promptness of the program in making payment for services

KEY (CORRECT ANSWERS)

1. B	11. C	21. D
2. A	12. A	22. D
3. C	13. C	23. C
4. D	14. D	24. A
5. A	15. A	25. C
6. D	16. C	
7. B	17. B	
8. C	18. C	
9. B	19. B	
10. D	20. A	

NAME AND NUMBER CHECKING
EXAMINATION SECTION
TEST 1

DIRECTIONS: This test is designed to measure your speed/and accuracy. You are urged to work both quickly and accurately and to do correctly as many lists as you can in the time allowed. The test consists of lists or pairs of names and numbers. Count the number of IDENTICAL pairs in each list. Then, select the correct number, 1, 2, 3, 4, 5, and indicate your choice in the space at the right. Two sample questions are presented for your guidance, together with the correct solutions.

SAMPLE LIST A
Adelphi College – Adelphia College
Braxton Corp – Braxeton Corp.
Wassaic State School – Wassaic State School
Central Islip State Hospital – Central Isllip State Hospital
Greenwich House – Greenwich House

NOTE: There are only two correct pairs—Wassaic State School and Greenwich House. Therefore, the CORRECT answer is 2.

SAMPLE LIST B
78453694 – 78453684
784530 – 784530
533 – 534
67845 – 67845
2368745 – 2368755

NOTE: There are only two correct pairs—784530 and 67845. Therefore, the CORRECT answer is 2.

LIST 1 1.____
    Diagnostic Clinic   – Diagnostic Clinic
    Yorkville Health   – Yorkville Health
    Meinhard Clinic   – Meinhart Clinic
    Corlears Clinic   – Carlears Clinic
    Tremont Diagnostic   – Tremont Diagnostic

LIST 2 2.____
    73526   – 73526
    7283627198   – 7283627198
    627   – 637
    728352617283   – 7283526178282
    6281   – 6281

2 (#1)

LIST 3
    Jefferson Clinic   – Jeffersen Clinic
    Mott Haven Center   – Mott Havan Center
    Bronx Hospital   – Bronx Hospital
    Montefiore Hospital   – Montifeore Hospital
    Beth Isreal Hospital   – Beth Israel Hospital

3.____

LIST 4
    936271826   – 936371826
    5271   – 5291
    82637192037   – 82637192037
    527182   – 5271882
    726354256   - 72635456

4.____

LIST 5
    Trinity Hospital   – Trinity Hospital
    Central Harlem   – Centrel Harlem
    St. Luke's Hospital   – St. Lukes' Hospital
    Mt. Sinai Hospital   – Mt. Sinia Hospital
    N.Y. Dispensery   – N.Y. Dispensary

5.____

LIST 6
    725361552637   – 725361555637
    7526378   – 7526377
    6975   – 6975
    82637481028   – 82637481028
    3427   – 3429

6.____

LIST 7
    Misericordia Hospital   – Miseracordia Hospital
    Lebonan Hospital   – Lebanon Hospital
    Gouverneur Hospital   – Gouverner Hospital
    German Polyclinic   – German Policlinic
    French Hospital   – French Hospital

7.____

LIST 8
    8277364933251   – 827364933351
    63728   – 63728
    367281   – 367281
    62733846273   – 6273846293
    62836   - 6283

8.____

LIST 9
    King's County Hospital   – Kings County Hospital
    St. Johns Long Island   – St. John's Long Island
    Bellevue Hospital   – Bellvue Hospital
    Beth David Hospital   – Beth David Hospital
    Samaritan Hospital   – Samariton Hospital

9.____

3 (#1)

LIST 10
    62836454   – 62836455
    42738267   – 42738369
    573829   – 573829
    738291627874   – 738291627874
    725   - 735

10.____

LIST 11
    Bloomingdal Clinic   – Bloomingdale Clinic
    Communitty Hospital   – Community Hospital
    Metroplitan Hospital   – Metropoliton Hospital
    Lenox Hill Hospital   – Lonex Hill Hospital
    Lincoln Hospital   – Lincoln Hospital

11.____

LIST 12
    6283364728   – 6283648
    627385   – 627383
    54283902   – 54283602
    63354   – 63354
    7283562781   - 7283562781

12.____

LIST 13
    Sydenham Hospital   – Sydanham Hospital
    Roosevalt Hospital   – Roosevelt Hospital
    Vanderbilt Clinic   – Vanderbild Clinic
    Women's Hospital   – Woman's Hospital
    Flushing Hospital   – Flushing Hospital

13.____

LIST 14
    62738   – 62738
    727355542321   – 72735542321
    263849332   – 263849332
    262837   – 263837
    47382912   - 47382922

14.____

LIST 15
    Episcopal Hospital   – Episcapal Hospital
    Flower Hospital   – Flouer Hospital
    Stuyvesent Clinic   – Stuyvesant Clinic
    Jamaica Clinic   – Jamaica Clinic
    Ridgwood Clinic   – Ridgewood Clinic

15.____

LIST 16
    628367299   – 628367399
    111   – 111
    118293304829   – 1182839489
    4448   – 4448
    333693678   - 333693678

16.____

4 (#1)

LIST 17   17._____
    Arietta Crane Farm   – Areitta Crane Farm
    Bikur Chilim Home   – Bikur Chilom Home
    Burke Foundation   – Burke Foundation
    Blythedale Home   – Blythdale Home
    Campbell Cottages   – Cambell Cottages

LIST 18   18._____
    32123   – 32132
    273893326783   – 27389326783
    473829   – 473829
    7382937   – 7383937
    3628890122332   - 36289012332

LIST 19   19._____
    Caraline Rest   – Caroline Rest
    Loreto Rest   – Loretto Rest
    Edgewater Creche   – Edgwater Creche
    Holiday Farm   – Holiday Farm
    House of St. Giles   – House of st. Giles

LIST 20   20._____
    557286777   – 55728677
    3678902   – 3678892
    1567839   – 1567839
    7865434712   – 7865344712
    9927382   - 9927382

LIST 21   21._____
    Isabella Home   – Isabela Home
    James A. Moore Home   – James A. More Home
    The Robin's Nest   – The Roben's Nest
    Pelham Home   – Pelam Home
    St. Eleanora's Home   – St. Eleanora's Home

LIST 22   22._____
    273648293048   – 273648293048
    334   – 334
    7362536478   – 7362536478
    7362819273   – 7362819273
    7362   - 7363

LIST 23   23._____
    St. Pheobe's Mission   – St. Phebe's Mission
    Seaside Home   – Seaside Home
    Speedwell Society   – Speedwell Society
    Valeria Home   – Valera Home
    Wiltwyck   - Wildwyck

5 (#1)

LIST 24
   63728   – 63738
   63728192736   – 63728192738
   428   – 458
   62738291527   – 62738291529
   63728192   - 63728192

24._____

LIST 25
   McGaffin   – McGafin
   David Ardslee   – David Ardslee
   Axton Supply   – Axeton Supply Co
   Alice Russell   – Alice Russell
   Dobson Mfg. Co. – Dobsen Mfg. Co.

25._____

KEY (CORRECT ANSWERS)

1.	3		11.	1
2.	3		12.	2
3.	1		13.	1
4.	1		14.	2
5.	1		15.	1
6.	2		16.	3
7.	1		17.	1
8.	2		18.	1
9.	1		19.	1
10.	2		20.	2

21. 1
22. 4
23. 2
24. 1
25. 2

TEST 2

DIRECTIONS: This test is designed to measure your speed/and accuracy. You are urged to work both quickly and accurately and to do correctly as many lists as you can in the time allowed. The test consists of lists or pairs of names and numbers. Count the number of IDENTICAL pairs in each list. Then, select the correct number, 1, 2, 3, 4, 5, and indicate your choice in the space at the right.

LIST 1   1.____
   82637381028   – 82637281028
   928   – 928
   72937281028   – 72937281028
   7362   – 7362
   927382615   – 927382615

LIST 2   2.____
   Albee Theatre   – Albee Theatre
   Lapland Lumber Co.   – Laplund Lumber Co.
   Adelphi College   – Adelphi College
   Jones & Son Inc.   – Jones & Sons Inc.
   S.W. Ponds Co.   – S.W. Ponds Co.

LIST 3   3.____
   85345   – 85345
   895643278   – 895643277
   726352   – 726353
   632685   – 632685
   7263524   – 7236524

LIST 4   4.____
   Eagle Library   – Eagle Library
   Dodge Ltd.   – Dodge Co.
   Stromberg Carlson   – Stromberg Carlsen
   Clairice Ling   – Clairice Linng
   Mason Book Co.   – Matson Book Co.

LIST 5   5.____
   66273   – 66273
   629   – 629
   7382517283   – 7382517283
   637281   – 639281
   2738261   – 2788261

LIST 6   6.____
   Robert MacColl   – Robert McColl
   Buick Motor   – Buck Motors
   Murray Bay & Co. Ltd.   – Murray Bay Co. Ltd.
   L.T. Ltyle   – L.T. Lyttle
   A.S. Landas   – A.S. Landas

2 (#2)

LIST 7
    6271526374890   – 627152637490
    73526189   – 73526189
    5372   – 5392
    637281142   – 63728124
    4783946   – 4783046

7.____

LIST 8
    Tyndall Burke   – Tyndell Burke
    W. Briehl   – W. Briehl
    Burritt Publishing Co.   – Buritt Publishing Co.
    Frederick Breyer & Co.   – Frederick Breyer Co.
    Bailey Buulard   – Bailey Bullard

8.____

LIST 9
    634   – 634
    16837   – 163837
    273892223678   – 27389223678
    527182   – 527782
    3628901223   – 3629002223

9.____

LIST 10
    Ernest Boas   – Ernest Boas
    Rankin Barne   – Rankin Barnes
    Edward Appley   – Edward Appely
    Camel   – Camel
    Caiger Food Co.   – Caiger Food Co.

10.____

LIST 11
    6273   – 6273
    322   – 332
    15672839   – 15672839
    63728192637   – 63728192639
    738   – 738

11.____

LIST 12
    Wells Fargo Co.   – Wells Fargo Co.
    W.D. Brett   – W.D. Britt
    Tassco Co.   – Tassko Co.
    Republic Mills   – Republic Mill
    R.W. Burnham   – R.W. Burhnam

12.____

LIST 13
    7253529152   – 7283529152
    6283   – 6383
    52839102738   – 5283910238
    308   – 398
    82637201927   – 8263720127

13.____

LIST 14
		14.____
Schumacker Co.	– Shumacker Co.	
C.H. Caiger	– C.H. Caiger	
Abraham Strauss	– Abram Straus	
B.F. Boettjer	– B.F. Boettijer	
Cut-Rate Store	– Cut-Rate Stores	

LIST 15
		15.____
15273826	– 15273826	
72537	– 73537	
726391027384	– 62639107384	
637389	– 627399	
725382910	– 725382910	

LIST 16
		16.____
Hixby Ltd.	– Hixby Lt'd.	
S. Reiner	– S. Riener	
Reynard Co.	– Reynord Co.	
Esso Gassoline Co.	– Esso Gasolene Co.	
Belle Brock	– Belle Brock	

LIST 17
		17.____
7245	– 7245	
819263728192	– 819263728172	
682537289	– 682537298	
789	– 789	
82936542891	– 82936542891	

LIST 18
		18.____
Joseph Cartwright	– Joseph Cartwrite	
Foote Food Co.	– Foot Food Co.	
Weiman & Held	– Weiman & Held	
Sanderson Shoe Co.	– Sandersen Shoe Co.	
A.M. Byrne	– A.N. Byrne	

LIST 19
		19.____
4738267	– 4738277	
63728	– 63729	
6283628901	– 6283628991	
918264	– 918264	
263728192037	– 2637728192073	

LIST 20
		20.____
Exray Laboratories	– Exray Labratories	
Curley Toy Co.	– Curly Toy Co.	
J. Lauer & Cross	– J. Laeur & Cross	
Mireco Brands	– Mireco Brands	
Sandor Lorand	– Sandor Larand	

4 (#2)

LIST 21
 607   – 609
 6405   – 6403
 976   – 996
 101267   – 101267
 2065432   – 20965432

21.____

LIST 22
 John Macy & Sons – John Macy & Son
 Venus Pencil Co. – Venus Pencil Co.
 Nell McGinnis   – Nell McGinnis
 McCutcheon & Co. – McCutcheon & Co.
 Sun-Tan Oil   – Sun-Tan Oil

22.____

LIST 23
 703345700   – 703345700
 46754   – 466754
 3367490   – 3367490
 3379   – 3778
 47384   – 47394

23.____

LIST 24
 arthritis   – arthritis
 asthma   – asthma
 endocrine   – endocrene
 gastro-enterological – gastrol-enteralogical
 orthopedic   – orthopedic

24.____

LIST 25
 743829432   – 743828432
 998   – 998
 732816253902 – 732816252902
 46829   – 46830
 7439120249   – 7439210249

25.____

KEY (CORRECT ANSWERS)

1.	4		11.	3
2.	3		12.	1
3.	2		13.	1
4.	1		14.	1
5.	2		15.	2
6.	1		16.	1
7.	2		17.	3
8.	1		18.	1
9.	1		19.	1
10.	3		20.	1

21. 1
22. 4
23. 2
24. 3
25. 1

———

NAME AND NUMBER COMPARISONS

COMMENTARY

This test seeks to measure your ability and disposition to do a job carefully and accurately, your attention to exactness and preciseness of detail, your alertness and versatility in discerning similarities and differences between things, and your power in systematically handling written language symbols.

It is actually a test of your ability to do academic and/or clerical work, using the basic elements of verbal (qualitative) and mathematical (quantitative) learning—words and numbers.

EXAMINATION SECTION

TEST 1

DIRECTIONS: In each line across the page there are three names or numbers that are much alike. Compare the three names or numbers and decide which ones are exactly alike. *PRINT IN THE SPACE AT THE RIGHT THE LETTER:*
  A. if all THREE names or numbers are exactly alike
  B. if only the FIRST and SECOND names or numbers are ALIKE
  C. if only the FIRST and THIRD names or numbers are alike
  D. if only the SECOND or THIRD names or numbers are alike
  E. if ALL THREE names or numbers are DIFFERENT

1.	Davis Hazen	David Hozen	David Hazen	1.____
2.	Lois Appel	Lois Appel	Lois Apfel	2.____
3.	June Allan	Jane Allan	Jane Allan	3.____
4.	10235	10235	10235	4.____
5.	32614	32164	32614	5.____

TEST 2

1.	2395890	2395890	2395890	1.____
2.	1926341	1926347	1926314	2.____
3.	E. Owens McVey	E. Owen McVey	E. Owen McVay	3.____
4.	Emily Neal Rouse	Emily Neal Rowse	Emily Neal Rowse	4.____
5.	H. Merritt Audubon	H. Merriott Audubon	H. Merritt Audubon	5.____

TEST 3

1.	6219354	6219354	6219354	1.____
2.	231793	2312793	2312793	2.____
3.	1065407	1065407	1065047	3.____
4.	Francis Ransdell	Frances Ramsdell	Francis Ramsdell	4.____
5.	Cornelius Detwiler	Cornelius Detwiler	Cornelius Detwiler	5.____

TEST 4

1.	6452054	6452564	6542054	1.____
2.	8501268	8501268	8501286	2.____
3.	Ella Burk Newham	Ella Burk Newnham	Elena Burk Newnham	3.____
4.	Jno. K. Ravencroft	Jno. H. Ravencroft	Jno. H. Ravencoft	4.____
5.	Martin Wills Pullen	Martin Wills Pulen	Martin Wills Pullen	5.____

TEST 5

1.	3457988	3457986	3457986	1.____
2.	4695682	4695862	4695682	2.____
3.	Stricklund Kaneydy	Sticklund Kanedy	Stricklund Kanedy	3.____
4.	Joy Harlor Witner	Joy Harloe Witner	Joy Harloe Witner	4.____
5.	R.M.O. Uberroth	R.M.O. Uberroth	R.N.O. Uberroth	5.____

3

TEST 6

1. 1592514	1592574	1592574	1._____
2. 2010202	2010202	2010220	2._____
3. 6177396	6177936	6177396	3._____
4. Drusilla S. Ridgeley	Drusilla S. Ridgeley	Drusilla S. Ridgeley	4._____
5. Andrei I. Tooumantzev	Andrei I. Tourmantzev	Andrei I. Toumantzov	5._____

TEST 7

1. 5261383	5261383	5261338	1._____
2. 8125690	8126690	8125609	2._____
3. W.E. Johnston	W.E. Johnson	W.E. Johnson	3._____
4. Vergil L. Muller	Vergil L. Muller	Vergil L. Muller	4._____
5. Atherton R. Warde	Asheton R. Warde	Atherton P. Warde	5._____

TEST 8

1. 013469.5	023469.5	02346.95	1._____
2. 33376	333766	333766	2._____
3. Ling-Temco-Vought	Ling-Tenco-Vought	Ling-Temco Vought	3._____
4. Lorilard Corp.	Lorillard Corp.	Lorrilard Corp.	4._____
5. American Agronomics Corporation	American Agronomics Corporation	American Agronomic Corporation	5._____

TEST 9

1.	436592864	436592864	436592864	1.____
2.	197765123	197755123	197755123	2.____
3.	Dewaay Cortvriendt International S.A.	Deway Cortvriendt International S.A.	Deway Corturiendt International S.A.	3.____
4.	Crédit Lyonnais	Crèdit Lyonnais	Crèdit Lyonais	4.____
5.	Algemene Bank Nederland N.V.	Algamene Bank Nederland N.V.	Algemene Bank Naderland N.V.	5.____

TEST 10

1.	00032572	0.0032572	00032522	1.____
2.	399745	399745	398745	2.____
3.	Banca Privata Finanziaria S.p.A.	Banca Privata Finanzaria S.P.A.	Banca Privata Finanziaria S.P.A.	3.____
4.	Eastman Dillon, Union Securities & Co.	Eastman Dillon, Union Securities Co.	Eastman Dillon, Union Securities & Co.	4.____
5.	Arnhold and S. Bleichroeder, Inc.	Arnhold & S. Bleichroeder, Inc.	Arnold and S. Bleichroeder, Inc.	5.____

TEST 11

DIRECTIONS: Answer the questions below on the basis of the following instructions: For each such numbered set of names, addresses, and numbers listed in Columns I and II, select your answer from the following options:
- A. The names in Columns I and II are different
- B. The addresses in Columns I and II are different
- C. The numbers in Columns I and II are different
- D. The names, addresses and numbers are identical

1. Francis Jones
   62 Stately Avenue
   96-12446

   Francis Jones
   62 Stately Avenue
   96-21446

   1.____

2. Julio Montez
   19 Ponderosa Road
   56-73161

   Julio Montez
   19 Ponderosa Road
   56-71361

   2.____

3. Mary Mitchell
   2314 Melbourne Drive
   68-92172

   Mary Mitchell
   2314 Melbourne Drive
   68-92172

   3.____

4. Harry Patterson
   25 Dunne Street
   14-33430

   Harry Patterson
   25 Dunne Street
   14-34330

   4.____

5. Patrick Murphy
   171 West Hosmer Street
   93-81214

   Patrick Murphy
   171 West Hosmer Street
   93-18214

   5.____

TEST 12

1. August Schultz
   816 St. Clair Avenue
   53-40149

2. George Taft
   72 Runnymede Street
   47-04033

3. Angus Henderson
   1418 Madison Street
   81-76375

4. Carolyn Mazur
   12 Rivenlew Road
   38-99615

5. Adele Russell
   1725 Lansing Lane
   72-91962

August Schultz
816 St. Claire Avenue
53-40149

George Taft
72 Runnymede Street
47-04023

Angus Henderson
1418 Madison Street
81-76375

Carolyn Mazur
12 Rivervane Road
38-99615

Adela Russell
1725 Lansing Lane
72-91962

1.____
2.____
3.____
4.____
5.____

TEST 13

DIRECTIONS: The following questions are based on the instructions given below. In each of the following questions, the 3-line name and address in Column I is the master-list entry, and the 3-line entry in Column II is the information to be checked against the master list.
If there is one line that is NOT exactly alike, mark your answer A.
If there are two lines NOT exactly alike, mark your answer B.
If there are three lines NOT exactly alike, mark your answer C.
If the lines ALL are exactly alike, mark your answer D.

1. Jerome A. Jackson
   1243 14th Avenue
   New York, N.Y. 10023

   Jerome A. Johnson
   1234 14th Avenue
   New York, N.Y. 10023
   1.____

2. Sophie Strachtheim
   33-28 Connecticut Ave.
   Far Rockaway, N.Y. 11697

   Sophie Strachtheim
   33-28 Connecticut Ave.
   Far Rockaway, N.Y. 11697
   2.____

3. Elisabeth NT. Gorrell
   256 Exchange St
   New York, N.Y. 10013

   Elizabeth NT. Correll
   256 Exchange St.
   New York, N.Y. 10013
   3.____

4. Maria J. Gonzalez
   7516 E. Sheepshead Rd.
   Brooklyn, N.Y. 11240

   Maria J. Gonzalez
   7516 N. Shepshead Rd.
   Brooklyn, N.Y. 11240
   4.____

5. Leslie B. Brautenweiler
   21-57A Seller Terr.
   Flushing, N.Y. 11367

   Leslie B. Brautenwieler
   21-75ASeiler Terr.
   Flushing, N.J. 11367
   5.____

KEY (CORRECT ANSWERS)

TEST 1	TEST 2	TEST 3	TEST 4	TEST 5	TEST 6	TEST 7
1. E	1. A	1. A	1. E	1. D	1. D	1. B
2. B	2. E	2. A	2. B	2. C	2. B	2. E
3. D	3. E	3. B	3. E	3. E	3. C	3. D
4. A	4. D	4. E	4. E	4. D	4. A	4. A
5. C	5. C	5. A	5. C	5. B	5. E	5. E

TEST 8	TEST 9	TEST 10	TEST 11	TEST 12	TEST 13
1. E	1. A	1. E	1. C	1. B	1. B
2. D	2. D	2. B	2. C	2. C	2. D
3. E	3. E	3. E	3. D	3. D	3. A
4. E	4. E	4. C	4. C	4. B	4. A
5. B	5. E	5. E	5. C	5. A	5. C

CODING

COMMENTARY

An ingenious question-type called coding, involving elements of alphabetizing, filing, name and number comparison, and evaluative judgment and application, has currently won wide acceptance in testing circles for measuring clerical aptitude and general ability, particularly on the senior (middle) grades (levels).

While the directions for this question usually vary in detail, the candidate is generally asked to consider groups of names, codes, and numbers, and, then, according to a given plan, to arrange codes in alphabetic order; to arrange these in numerical sequence; to re-arrange columns of names and numbers in correct order; to espy errors in coding; to choose the correct coding arrangement in consonance with the given directions and examples, etc.

This question-type appears to have few paramaters in respect to form, substance, or degree of difficulty.

Accordingly, acquaintance with, and practice in, the coding question is recommended for the serious candidate.

EXAMINATION SECTION
TEST 1

DIRECTIONS:

```
                                   CODE TABLE
   Name of Applicant      H A N G S B R U K E
   Test Code              c o m p l e x i t y
   File Number            0 1 2 3 4 5 6 7 8 9
```

Assume that each of the above *capital letters* is the first letter of the Name of an Applicant, that the *small letter* directly beneath each capital letter is the Test Code for the Applicant, and that the *number* directly beneath each code letter is the File Number for the Applicant.
In each of the following questions, the test code letters and the file numbers in Columns 2 and 3 should correspond to the capital letters in Column 1. For each question, look at each column carefully and mark your answer as follows:

If there is an error only in Column 2, mark your answer A.
If there is an error only in Column 3, mark your answer B.
If there is an error in both Columns 2 and 3, mark your answer C.
If both Columns 2 and 3 are correct, mark your answer D.

The following sample question is given to help you understand the procedure.

SAMPLE QUESTION

Column 1	Column 2	Column 3
AKEHN	otyci	18902

2 (#1)

In Column 2, the final test code letter "i" should be "m." Column 3 is correctly coded to Column 1. Since there is an error only in Column 2, the answer is A

	Column 1	Column 2	Column 3	
1.	NEKKU	mytti	29987	1.__
2.	KRAEB	txlye	86095	2.__
3.	ENAUK	ymoit	92178	3.__
4.	REANA	xeomo	69121	4.__
5.	EKHSE	ytcxy	97049	5.__

KEY (CORRECT ANSWERS)

1. B
2. C
3. D
4. A
5. C

TEST 2

DIRECTIONS: The employee identification codes in Column I begin and end with a capital letter and have an eight-digit number in between. In Questions 1 through 8, employee identification codes in Column I are to be arranged according to the following rules:

First: Arrange in alphabetical order according to the first letter.

Second: When two or more employee identification codes have the same first letter, arrange in alphabetical order according to the last letter.

Third: When two or more employee codes have the same first and last letters, arrange in numerical order beginning with the lowest number.

The employee identification codes in Column I are numbered 1 through 5 in the order in which they are listed. In Column II the numbers 1 through 5 are arranged in four different ways to show different arrangements of the corresponding employee identification numbers. Choose the answer in Column II in which the employee identification numbers are arranged according to the above rules.

SAMPLE QUESTION

Column I
1. E75044127B
2. B96399104A
3. B93939086A
4. B47064465H
5. B99040922A

Column II
A. 4, 1, 3, 2, 5
B. 4, 1, 2, 3, 5
C. 4, 3, 2, 5, 1
D. 3, 2, 5, 4, 1

In the sample question, the four employee identification codes starting with B should be put before the employee identification code starting with E. The employee identification codes starting with B and ending with A should be put before the employee identification codes starting with B and ending with H. The three employee identification codes starting with B and ending with A should be listed in numerical order, beginning with the lowest number. The correct way to arrange the employee identification codes, therefore, is 3, 2, 5, 4, 1 shown below.

3. B93939086A
2. B96399104A
5. B99040922A
4. B47064465H
1. E75044127B

Therefore, the answer to the sample question is D. Now answer the following questions according to the above rules.

Column I

1.
1. G42786441J
2. H45665413J
3. G43117690J
4. G435466981
5. G416799421

Column II

A. 2, 5, 4, 3, 1
B. 5, 4, 1, 3, 2
C. 4, 5, 1, 3, 2
D. 1, 3, 5, 4, 2

1._____

2 (#2)

2.
1. S44556178T
2. T43457169T
3. S53321176T
4. T53317998S
5. S67673942S

A. 1, 3, 5, 2, 4
B. 4, 3, 5, 2, 1
C. 5, 3, 1, 2, 4
D. 5, 1, 3, 4, 2

2._____

3.
1. R63394217D
2. R63931247D
3. R53931247D
4. R66874239D
4. R46799366D

A. 5, 4, 2, 3, 1
B. 1, 5, 3, 2, 4
C. 5, 3, 1, 2, 4
D. 5, 1, 2, 3, 4

3._____

4.
1. A35671968B
2. A35421794C
3. A35466987B
4. C10435779A
5. C00634779B

A. 3, 2, 1, 4, 5
B. 2, 3, 1, 5, 4
C. 1, 3, 2, 4, 5
D. 3, 1, 2, 4, 5

4._____

5.
1. I99746426Q
2. I10445311Q
3. J63749877P
4. J03421739Q
5. J00765311Q

A. 2, 1, 3, 5, 4
B. 5, 4, 2, 1, 3
C. 4, 5, 3, 2, 1
D. 2, 1, 4, 5, 3

5._____

6.
1. M33964217N
2. N33942770N
3. N06155881M
4. M00433669M
5. M79034577N

A. 4, 1, 5, 2, 3
B. 5, 1, 4, 3, 2
C. 4, 1, 5, 3, 2
D. 1, 4, 5, 2, 3

6._____

7.
1. D77643905C
2. D44106788C
3. D13976022F
4. D97655430E
5. D00439776F

A. 1, 2, 5, 3, 4
B. 5, 3, 2, 1, 4
C. 2, 1, 5, 3, 4
D. 2, 1, 4, 5, 3

7._____

8.
1. W22746920A
2. W22743720A
3. W32987655A
4. W43298765A
5. W30987433A

A. 2, 1, 3, 4, 5
B. 2, 1, 5, 3, 4
C. 1, 2, 3, 4, 5
D. 1, 2, 5, 3, 4

8._____

KEY (CORRECT ANSWERS)

1. B
2. D
3. C
4. D
5. A
6. C
7. D
8. B

TEST 3

DIRECTIONS: Each of the following equestions consists of three sets of names and name codes. In each question, the two names and name codes on the same line are supposed to be exactly the same.

Look carefully at each set of names and codes and mark your answer:
- A. if there are mistakes in all three sets
- B. if there are mistakes in two of the sets
- C. if there is a mistake in only one set
- D. if there are no mistakes in any of the sets

The following sample question is given to help you understand the procedure.

Macabe, John N. - V 53162	Macade, John N. - V 53162
Howard, Joan S. - J 24791	Howard, Joan S. - J 24791
Ware, Susan B. - A 45068	Ware, Susan B. - A 45968

In the above sample question, the names and name codes of the first set are not exactly the same because of the spelling of the last name (Macabe - Macade). The names and name codes of the second set are exactly the same. The names and name codes of the third set are not exactly the same because the two name codes are different (A 45068 - A 45968), Since there are mistakes in only 2 of the sets, the answer to the sample question is B.

1. Powell, Michael C. - 78537 F   Powell, Michael C. - 78537 F   1.____
   Martinez, Pablo, J. - 24435 P   Martinez, Pablo J. - 24435 P
   MacBane, Eliot M. - 98674 E   MacBane, Eliot M. - 98674 E

2. Fitz-Kramer Machines Inc. - 259090   Fitz-Kramer Machines Inc. - 259090   2.____
   Marvel Cleaning Service - 482657   Marvel Cleaning Service - 482657
   Donate, Carl G. - 637418   Danato, Carl G. - 687418

3. Martin Davison Trading Corp. - 43108 T   Martin Davidson Trading Corp. - 43108 T   3.____
   Cotwald Lighting Fixtures - 76065 L   Cotwald Lighting Fixtures - 70056 L
   R. Crawford Plumbers - 23157 C   R. Crawford Plumbers - 23157 G

4. Fraiman Engineering Corp. - M4773   Friaman Engineering Corp. -M4773   4.____
   Neuman, Walter B. - N7745   Neumen, Walter B. - N7745
   Pierce, Eric M. - W6304   Pierce, Eric M. - W6304

5. Constable, Eugene - B 64837   Comstable, Eugene - B 64837   5.____
   Derrick, Paul - H 27119   Derrik, Paul - H 27119
   Heller, Karen - S 49606   Heller, Karen - S 46906

6. Hernando Delivery Service Co. - D 7456   Hernando Delivery Service Co. - D 7456   6.____
   Barettz Electrical Supplies - N 5392   Barettz Electrical Supplies - N 5392
   Tanner, Abraham - M 4798   Tanner, Abraham - M 4798

7. Kalin Associates - R 38641   Kaline Associates - R 38641   7.____
   Sealey, Robert E. - P 63533   Sealey, Robert E. - P 63553
   Scalsi Office Furniture   Scalsi Office Furniture

8. Janowsky, Philip M.- 742213
Hansen, Thomas H. - 934816
L. Lester and Son Inc. - 294568

Janowsky, Philip M.- 742213
Hanson, Thomas H. - 934816
L. Lester and Son Inc. - 294568

8.____

KEY (CORRECT ANSWERS)

1. D
2. C
3. A
4. B
5. A

6. D
7. B
8. C

TEST 4

DIRECTIONS: The following questions are to be answered on the basis of the following Code Table. In this table, for each number, a corresponding code letter is given. Each of the questions contains three pairs of numbers and code letters. In each pair, the code letters should correspond with the numbers in accordance with the Code Table.

CODE TABLE

Number	1	2	3	4	5	6	7	8	9	0
Corresponding Code Letter	Y	N	Z	X	W	T	U	P	S	R

In some of the pairs below, an error exists in the coding. Examine the pairs in each question carefully. If an error exists in:
    Only one of the pairs in the question, mark your answer A.
    Any two pairs in the question, mark your answer B.
    All three pairs in the question, mark your answer C.
    None of the pairs in the question, mark your answer D.

SAMPLE QUESTION

37258	-	ZUNWP
948764	-	SXPTTX
73196	-	UZYSP

In the above sample, the first pair is correct since each number, as listed, has the correct corresponding code letter. In the second pair, an error exists because the number 7 should have the code letter U instead of the letter T. In the third pair, an error exists because the number 6 should have the code letter T instead of the letter P. Since there are errors in two of the three pairs, the correct answer is B.

1. 493785   - XSZUPW
   86398207   - PTUSPNRU
   5943162   - WSXZYTN

2. 5413968412   - WXYZSTPXYR
   8763451297   - PUTZXWYZSU
   4781965302   - XUPYSUWZRN

3. 79137584   - USYRUWPX
   638247   - TZPNXS
   49679312   - XSTUSZYN

4. 37854296   - ZUPWXNST
   09183298   - RSYXZNSP
   91762358   - SYUTNXWP

5. 3918762485   - ZSYPUTNXPW
   1578291436   - YWUPNSYXZT
   2791385674   - NUSYZPWTUX

2 (#4)

6. 197546821 - YSUWSTPNY   6.____
   873024867 - PUZRNWPTU
   583179246 - WPZYURNXT

7. 510782463 - WYRUSNXTZ   7.____
   478192356 - XUPYSNZWT
   961728532 - STYUNPWXN

KEY (CORRECT ANSWERS)

1. A
2. C
3. B
4. B
5. D

6. C
7. B

TEST 5

DIRECTIONS: Assume that each of the capital letters is the first letter of the name of a city using EAM equipment. The number directly beneath each capital letter is the code number for the city. The small letter beneath each code number is the code letter for the number of EAM divisions in the city and the + or - symbol directly beneath each code letter is the code symbol which signifies whether or not the city uses third generation computers with the EAM equipment.

The questions that follow show City Letters in Column I, Code Numbers in Column II, Code Letters in Column III, and Code Symbols in Column IV. If correct. each City Letter in Column I should correspond by position with each of the three codes shown in the other three columns, in accordance with the coding key shown. BUT there are some errors. For each question,

If there is a total of ONE error in Columns 2, 3, and 4, mark your answer A.
If there is a total of TWO errors in Columns 2, 3, and 4, mark your answer B.
If there is a total of THREE errors in Columns 2, 3, and 4, mark your answer C.
If Columns 2, 3, and 4 are correct, mark your answer D.

SAMPLE QUESTION

I	II	III	IV
City Letter	Code Numbers	Code Letters	Code Symbols
Y J M O S	5 3 7 9 8	e b g i h	- - + + -

The errors are as follows: In Column 2, the Code Number should be "2" instead of "3" for City Letter "J," and in Column 4 the Code Symbol should be "+" instead of "-" for City Letter "Y." Since there is a total of two errors in Columns 2, 3, and 4, the answer to this sample question is B.

Now answer questions 1 through 9 according to these rules.

CODING KEY

City	Letter	P	J	R	T	Y	K	M	S	0
Code	Number	1	2	3	4	5	6	7	8	9
Code	Letter	a	b	c	d	e	f	g	h	i
Code	Symbol	+	-	+	-	+	-	+	-	+

	I City Letters	II Code Numbers	III Code Letters	IV Code Symbols	
1.	K O R M P	6 9 3 7 1	f i e g a	- - + + +	1._____
2.	O T P S Y	9 4 1 8 6	b d a h e	+ - - - +	2._____
3.	R S J T M	3 8 1 4 7	c h b e g	- - - - +	3._____
4.	P M S K J	1 7 8 6 2	a g h f b	+ + - - -	4._____
5.	M Y T J R	7 5 4 2 3	g e d f c	+ + - - +	5._____
6.	T P K Y O	4 1 6 7 9	d a f e i	- + - + -	6._____
7.	S K O R T	8 6 9 3 5	h f i c d	- - + + -	7._____
8.	J R Y P K	2 3 5 1 9	b d e a f	- + + + -	8._____
9.	R O M P Y	4 9 7 1 5	c i g a d	+ + - + +	9._____

KEY (CORRECT ANSWERS)

1. B
2. C
3. C
4. D
5. A

6. B
7. A
8. B
9. C

TEST 6

Assume that each of the capital letters is the first letter of the name of an offense, that the small letter directly beneath each capital letter is the code letter for the offense, and that the number directly beneath each code letter is the file number for the offense.

DIRECTIONS: In each of the following questions, the code letters and file numbers should correspond to the capital letters.

If there is an error only in Column 2, mark your answer A.
If there is an error only in Column 3, mark your answer B.
If there is an error in both Column 2 and Column 3, mark your answer C.
If both Columns 2 and 3 are correct, mark your answer D.

SAMPLE QUESTION

Column 1	Column 2	Column 3
BNARGHSVVU	emoxtylcci	6357905118

The code letters in Column 2 are correct but the first "5" in Column 3 should be "2." Therefore, the answer is B. Now answer the following questions according to the above rules.

CODE TABLE

Name of Offense	V	A	N	D	S	B	R	U	G	H
Code Letter	c	o	m	p	l	e	x	i	t	y
File Number	1	2	3	4	5	6	7	8	9	0

	Column 1	Column 2	Column 3	
1.	HGDSBNBSVR	ytplxmelcx	0945736517	1.____
2.	SDGUUNHVAH	lptiimycoy	5498830120	2.____
3.	BRSNAAVUDU	exlmooctpi	6753221848	3.____
4.	VSRUDNADUS	cleipmopil	1568432485	4.____
5.	NDSHVRBUAG	mplycxeiot	3450175829	5.____
6.	GHUSNVBRDA	tyilmcexpo	9085316742	6.____
7.	DBSHVURANG	pesycixomt	4650187239	7.____
8.	RHNNASBDGU	xymnolepti	7033256398	8.____

KEY (CORRECT ANSWERS)

1. C
2. D
3. A
4. C
5. B

6. D
7. A
8. C

TEST 7

DIRECTIONS: Each of the following questions contains three sets of code letters and code numbers. In each set, the code numbers should correspond with the code letters as given in the Table, but there is a coding error in some of the sets. Examine the sets in each question carefully.

Mark your answer A if there is a coding error in only *ONE* of the sets in the question.
Mark your answer B if there is a coding error in any *TWO* of the sets in the question.
Mark your answer C if there is a coding error in all *THREE* sets in the question.
Mark your answer D if there is a coding error in *NONE* of the sets in the question.

SAMPLE QUESTION

fgzduwaf - 35720843
uabsdgfw - 04262538
hhfaudgs - 99340257

In the above sample question, the first set is right because each code number matches the code letter as in the Code Table. In the second set, the corresponding number for the code letter b is wrong because it should be 1 instead of 2. In the third set, the corresponding number for the last code letter s is wrong because it should be 6 instead of 7. Since there is an error in two of the sets, the answer to the above sample question is B.

In the Code Table below, each code letter has a corresponding code number directly beneath it.

CODE TABLE

Code Letter	b	d	f	a	g	s	z	w	h	u
Code Number	1	2	3	4	5	6	7	8	9	0

1. fsbughwz - 36104987   zwubgasz - 78025467   1._____
   ghgufddb - 59583221

2. hafgdaas - 94351446   ddsfabsd - 22734162   2._____
   wgdbssgf - 85216553

3. abfbssbd - 41316712   ghzfaubs - 59734017   3._____
   sdbzfwza - 62173874

4. whfbdzag - 89412745   daaszuub - 24467001   4._____
   uzhfwssd - 07936623

5. zbadgbuh - 71425109   dzadbbsz - 27421167   5._____
   gazhwaff - 54798433

6. fbfuadsh - 31304265   gzfuwzsb - 57300671   6._____
   bashhgag - 14699535

KEY (CORRECT ANSWERS)

1. B
2. C
3. B
4. B
5. D
6. C

TEST 8

DIRECTIONS: The following questions are to be answered on the basis of the following Code Table. In this table every letter has a corresponding code number to be punched. Each question contains three pairs of letters and code numbers. In each pair, the code numbers should correspond with the letters in accordance with the Code Table.

CODE TABLE

Letter	P	L	A	N	D	C	O	B	U	R
Corresponding Code Number	1	2	3	4	5	6	7	8	9	0

In some of the pairs below, an error exists in the coding. Examine the pairs in each question. Mark your answer

A if there is a mistake in only *one* of the pairs
B if there is a mistake in only *two* of the pairs
C if there is a mistake in *all three* of the pairs
D if there is a mistake in *none* of the pairs

SAMPLE QUESTION

LCBPUPAB - 26819138
ACOABOL - 3683872
NDURONUC - 46901496

In the above sample, the first pair is correct since each letter as listed has the correct corresponding code number. In the second pair, an error exists because the letter O should have the code number 7, instead of 8. In the third pair, an error exists because the letter D should have the code number 5, instead of 6. Since there are errors in two of the three pairs, your answer should be B.

1. ADCANPLC - 35635126   DORURBBO - 57090877   1.____
   PNACBUCP - 14368061

2. LCOBLRAP - 26782931   UPANUPCD - 91349156   2.____
   RLDACLRO - 02536207

3. LCOROPAR - 26707130   BALANRUP - 83234091   3.____
   DOPOAULL - 57173922

4. ONCRUBAP - 74609831   DCLANORD - 56243705   4.____
   AORPDUR - 3771590

5. PANRBUCD - 13408965   UAOCDPLR - 93765120   5.____
   OPDDOBRA - 71556803

6. BAROLDCP - 83072561   PNOCOBLA - 14767823   6.____
   BURPDOLA - 89015723

7. ANNCPABO - 34461387   DBALDRCP - 58325061   7.____
   ACRPOUL - 3601792

95

2 (#8)

8. BLAPOUR - 8321790 NOACNPL - 4736412 8.____
   RODACORD - 07536805

9. ADUBURCL - 3598062 NOCOBAPR - 47578310 9.____
   PRONDALU - 10754329

10. UBADCLOR - 98356270 NBUPPARA - 48911033 10.____
    LONDUPRC - 27459106

KEY (CORRECT ANSWERS)

1. C
2. B
3. D
4. B
5. A

6. D
7. B
8. B
9. C
10. A

TEST 9

DIRECTIONS: Answer questions 1 through 10 ONLY on the basis of the following information.
Column I consists of serial numbers of dollar bills. Column II shows different ways of arranging the corresponding serial numbers.

The serial numbers of dollar bills in Column I begin and end with a capital letter and have an eight-digit number in between. The serial numbers in Column I are to be arranged according to the following rules:

FIRST: In alphabetical order according to the first letter.

SECOND: When two or more serial numbers have the same first letter, in alphabetical order according to the last letter.

THIRD: When two or more serial numbers have the same first and last letters, in numerical order, beginning with the lowest number.

The serial numbers in Column I are numbered (1) through (5) in the order in which they are listed. In Column II the numbers (1) through (5) are arranged in four different ways to show different arrangements of the corresponding serial numbers. Choose the answer in Column II in which the serial numbers are arranged according to the above rules.

SAMPLE QUESTION

	COLUMN I		COLUMN II
(1)	E75044127B	(A)	4, 1, 3, 2, 5
(2)	B96399104A	(B)	4, 1, 2, 3, 5
(3)	B93939086A	(C)	4, 3, 2, 5, 1
(4)	B47064465H	(D)	3, 2, 5, 4, 1
(5)	B99040922A		

In the sample question, the four serial numbers starting with B should be put before the serial number starting with E. The serial numbers starting with B and ending with A should be put before the serial number starting with B and ending with H. The three serial numbers starting with B and ending with A should be listed in numerical order, beginning with the lowest number. The correct way to arrange the serial numbers, therefore, is:

(3)	B93939086A
(2)	B96399104A
(5)	B99040922A
(4)	B47064465H
(1)	E75044127B

Since the order of arrangement is 3, 2, 5, 4, 1, the answer to the sample question is (D).

		COLUMN I			COLUMN II
1.	(1)	P44343314Y	A.	2, 3, 1, 4, 5
	(2)	P44141341S	B.	1, 5, 3, 2, 4
	(3)	P44141431L	C.	4, 2, 3, 5, 1
	(4)	P41143413W	D.	5, 3, 2, 4, 1
	(5)	P44313433H		
2.	(1)	D89077275M	A.	3, 2, 5, 4, 1
	(2)	D98073724N	B.	1, 4, 3, 2, 5
	(3)	D90877274N	C.	4, 1, 5, 2, 3
	(4)	D98877275M	D.	1, 3, 2, 5, 4
	(5)	D98873725N		

2 (#9)

3.	(1)	H32548137E		A.	2,	4,	5,	1,	3
	(2)	H35243178A		B.	1,	5,	2,	3,	4
	(3)	H35284378F		C.	1,	5,	2,	4,	3
	(4)	H35288337A		D.	2,	1,	5,	3,	4
	(5)	H32883173B							
4.	(1)	K24165039H		A.	4,	2,	5,	3,	1
	(2)	F24106599A		B.	2,	3,	4,	1,	5
	(3)	L21406639G		C.	4,	2,	5,	1,	3
	(4)	C24156093A		D.	1,	3,	4,	5,	2
	(5)	K24165593D							
5.	(1)	H79110642E		A.	2,	1,	3,	5,	4
	(2)	H79101928E		B.	2,	1,	4,	5,	3
	(3)	A79111567F		C.	3,	5,	2,	1,	4
	(4)	H79111796E		D.	4,	3,	5,	1,	2
	(5)	A79111618F							
6.	(1)	P16388385W		A.	3,	4,	5,	2,	1
	(2)	R16388335V		B.	2,	3,	4,	5,	1
	(3)	P16383835W		C.	2,	4,	3,	1,	5
	(4)	R18386865V		D.	3,	1,	5,	2,	4
	(5)	P18686865W							
7.	(1)	B42271749G		A.	4,	1,	5,	2,	3
	(2)	B42271779G		B.	4,	1,	2,	5,	3
	(3)	E43217779G		C.	1,	2,	4,	5,	3
	(4)	B42874119C		D.	5,	3,	1,	2,	4
	(5)	E42817749G							
8.	(1)	M57906455S		A.	4,	1,	5,	3,	2
	(2)	N87077758S		B.	3,	4,	1,	5,	2
	(3)	N87707757B		C.	4,	1,	5,	2,	3
	(4)	M57877759B		D.	1,	5,	3,	2,	4
	(5)	M57906555S							
9.	(1)	C69336894Y		A.	2,	5,	3,	1,	4
	(2)	C69336684V		B.	3,	2,	5,	1,	4
	(3)	C69366887W		C.	3,	1,	4,	5,	2
	(4)	C69366994Y		D.	2,	5,	1,	3,	4
	(5)	C69336865V							
10.	(1)	A56247181D		A.	1,	5,	3,	2,	4
	(2)	A56272128P		B.	3,	1,	5,	2,	4
	(3)	H56247128D		C.	3,	2,	1,	5,	4
	(4)	H56272288P		D.	1,	5,	2,	3,	4
	(5)	A56247188D							

KEY (CORRECT ANSWERS)

1. D   6. D
2. B   7. B
3. A   8. A
4. C   9. A
5. C   10. D

TEST 10

DIRECTIONS: Answer the following questions on the basis of the instructions, the code, and the sample questions given below. Assume that an officer at a certain location is equipped with a two-way radio to keep him in constant touch with his security headquarters. Radio messages and replies are given in code form, as follows:

CODE TABLE

Radio Code for Situation	J	P	M	F	B
Radio Code for Action to be Taken	o	r	a	z	q
Radio Response for Action Being Taken	1	2	3	4	5

Assume that each of the above capital letters is the radio code for a particular type of situation, that the small letter below each capital letter is the radio code for the action an officer is directed to take, and that the number directly below each small letter is the radio response an officer should make to indicate what action was actually taken.

In each of the following questions, the code letter for the action directed (Column 2) and the code number for the action taken (Column 3) should correspond to the capital letters in Column 1.

INSTRUCTIONS: If only Column 2 is different from Column 1, mark your answer I.
If only Column 3 is different from Column 1, mark your answer II.
If both Column 2 and Column 3 are different from Column I, mark your answer III.
If both Columns 2 and 3 are the same as Column 1, mark your answer IV.

SAMPLE QUESTION

Column 1	Column 2	Column 3
JPFMB	orzaq	12453

The CORRECT answer is: A. I B. II C. III D. IV

The code letters in Column 2 are correct, but the numbers "53" in Column 3 should be "35." Therefore, the answer is B. Now answe the following questions according to the above rules.

	Column 1	Column 2	Column 3	
1.	PBFJM	rqzoa	25413	1._____
2.	MPFBJ	zrqao	32541	2._____
3.	JBFPM	oqzra	15432	3._____
4.	BJPMF	qaroz	51234	4._____
5.	PJFMB	rozaq	21435	5._____
6.	FJBMP	zoqra	41532	6._____

KEY (CORRECT ANSWERS)

1. D
2. C
3. B
4. A
5. D
6. A

MEDICAL/NURSING SCIENCE

TABLES OF ABBREVIATIONS

1. GENERAL

@	at
A	admitted to hospital
aa	of each
abd	abdomen
a.c.	before meals
ad lib	as desired
AFB	acid fast bacillus
am	morning
amp	ampule
amt	amount
AOW	admitted from other ward
Ba. E.	barium enema
b.i.d	twice a day
BMR	basal metabolic rate
BP	blood pressure
BSP	bromsulphalein
BUN	blood urea nitrogen
C	centigrade
$\bar{C}$	with
Ca	calcium
Cap	capacity beds, capsule
Cath	catheterize
CBC	complete blood count
Cc	cubic centimeter
Cl	chloride
CLR	census last report
cm	centimeter
comp	compound
CO_2 vol. %	carbon dioxide volume
CSR	central supply room or central dressing room
C and S	culture and sensitivity
D	discharged from hospital
DD	discharged by death
DC	discontinued
diff	differential count
DOA	dead on arrival
DOS	day of surgery
dr	dram
Dr	doctor
D/NS or D/S	dextrose in normal saline
D/W	dextrose in water
ECG or EKG	electrocardiogram
EEG	electroencephalogram
EENT	eye, ear, nose and throat

GENERAL (CONTINUED)

elix	elixir
exam	examination
ext	extract
F	fahrenheit
FBS	fasting blood sugar
Fe	iron
Fr	French, denotes size of catheter or tube
ft	feet, foot
GB	gallbladder
GI	gastrointestinal
Gm	gram
gr	grain
GTT	glucose tolerance test
gtt	drop/drops
GU	genitourinary
GYN	gynecology
"H." or S.C	hypodermic/subcutaneous
h. or hr	hour
hgb	hemoglobin
Hg	mercury
HP	head privileges
HS or hs	at bedtime
ht	height
HCl	hydrochloric acid
IM	intramuscular
I and O	intake and output
in	inch
I.V	intravenous
IVP	intravenous pyelogram
K	potassium
KCl	potassium chloride
kg	kilogram
L	leave or liberty
Lab	laboratory
LLL	left lower lobe
LLQ	left lower quadrant
LP	lumbar puncture
LUL	left upper lobe
LUQ	left upper quadrant
m	minim
mcg	microgram
Med	medical, medicine
mEg	milliequivalent
mg. or mgm	milligram, one thousandth of a gram

GENERAL (CONTINUED)

ml	milliliter
min	minute, minim
mm	millimeter
Na	sodium
NaCl	sodium chloride
no	number
NP	neuropsychiatric
NPN	non protéine nitrogène
NPO	nothing by mouth
NSS or NS	normal saline solution
OB	obstetrical or maternity
O_2	oxygen
oint	ointment
OOD	Officer of the Day
OR	operating room
OPD	outpatient department
OT	occupational therapy
oz	ounce
P.	phosphorus
P	pulse
PAL	prisoner at large
P.B.I	protein bound iodine
Ped	pediatrics or children
p.c	after meals
Pharm	pharmacy
p.m	afternoon, evening
p.o	by mouth
POD	postoperative day
Postop	after surgery
P.P.D	purified protein derivative
p.r.n	when necessary
Preop	before surgery
PSP	phenolsulfonphthalein
PT	physical therapy
pt	patient/pint
q	every
q.d	every day
q.h	every hour
q. 2 h	every 2 hours
q. 2 h	every 3 hours
q. 4 h	every 4 hours
q.i.d	four time a day
q.n	every night
q.s	a sufficient quantity

GENERAL (CONTINUED)

qt	quart
R	respiration, rectal, right
R and M	routine and microscopic
RBC	red blood count
RLL	right lower lobe
RLQ	right lower quadrant
RML	right middle lobe
RUL	right upper lobe
RUQ	right upper quadrant without
SAE/SO	subsisting at home/out
S.C. or subcut	subcutaneous/hypodermic
Sed. rate	sedimentation rate
SL	serious list
sol	solution
SOQ	sick officers' quarters
Sp	spirit
spec	specimen
sp.gr	specific gravity
ss	half
S.S.E	soap solution enema
stat	immediately
Surg	surgical
T	temperature
Tab	tablet
TB	tuberculosis
T. or tbsp	tablespoon
t.i.d	three times a day
tinct. or tr	tincture
TOW	transfer to other ward
T.P.R	temperature, pulse, respiration
t. or tsp	teaspoon
U	unit
U.A	Unauthorized Absence
Vac	vacant beds
VSL	Very Serious List
WBC	white blood count
Wd	ward
wt	weight

2. WARD ADMINISTRATION

(NURSING NOTES, DOCTOR'S ORDERS, AND WARD RECORDS)

A	admitted to hospital
abd	abdomen
a.m	morning
amt	amount
AOW	admitted from other ward
BP	blood pressure
C	centigrade
cap	capacity
CLR	census last report
CSR	central supply room
D	discharged from hospital
DD	discharged by death
DOA	dead on arrival
DOS	day of surgery
Dr	doctor
E.E.N T	eye, ear, nose, and throat
exam	examination
F	fahrenheit
Fr	French, denotes size of catheter or tube
ft	feet, foot
GU	genitourinary
GYN	gynecology
HP	head privileges
ht	height
I&O	intake and output
in	inch
kg	kilogram
L	leave or liberty
LLL	left lower lobe
LLQ	left lower quadrant
LP	lumbar puncture
LUL	left upper lobe
LUQ	left upper quadrant
Med	medical, medicine
no	number
NP	neuropsychiatric
NPO	nothing by mouth
OB	obstetrics
occ	occupied
OOD	officer of the day
OR	operating room
OPD	outpatient department
OT	occupational therapy

WARD ADMINISTRATION (CONTINUED)

P	Pulse
PAL	prisoner at large
Ped	pediatrics or children
Pharm	pharmacy
p.m	afternoon, evening
POD	postoperative day
Postop	after surgery
Preop	before surgery
PT	physical therapy
pt	patient
R	respiration, rectal, right
RLL	right lower lobe
RLQ	right lower quadrant
RML	right middle lobe
RUL	right upper lobe
RUQ	right upper quadrant
SAH/SO	subsisting at home/out
SL	serious list
SOQ	sick officers' quarters
Surg	surgical
T	temperature
TB	tuberculosis
TOW	transfer to other ward
T.P.R	temperature, pulse, and respiration
UA	unauthorized absence
Vac	vacant beds
VSL	very serious list
Wd	ward
wt	weight

3. MEDICATIONS/TREATMENTS

@	at
$\overline{aa}$	
a.c	before meals
ad lib	as desired
amp	ampule
b.i.d	twice a day
$\overline{c}$	with
Ca	calcium
cap	capsule
cath	catheterize
cc	cubic centimeter
Cl	chloride
cm	centimeter
comp	compound
DC	discontinued
dr	dram
D/NS or D S	dextrose in normal saline
D/W	dextrose in water
elix	elixir
ext	extract
Fe	iron
Gm	gram
gr	grain
gt./gtt	drop/drops
"H" or S.C	hypodermic/subcutaneous
h. or hr	hour
Hg	mercury
HS or hs	at bedtime
HCl	hydrocloric acid
IM	intramuscular
I.V	intravenous
K	potassium
KCl	potassium chloride
M	minim
mcg	microgram
mEq	milliequivalent
mg. or mgm	milligram
ml	milliliter
min	minute
mm	millimeter
Na	sodium
NaCl	sodium chloride
NSS or NS	normal saline solution
O_2	oxygen
oint	ointment
oz	ounce
P	phosphorus
p.c	after meals

MEDICATIONS/TREATMENTS (CONTINUED)

p.o	by mouth
p.r.n	when necessary
pt	pint
q	every
q.d	every day
q.h	every hour
q. 2h	every 2 hours
q. 3h	every 3 hours
q. 4h	every 4 hours
q.i.d	four times a day
q.n	every night
q.s	a sufficient quantity
qt	quart
$\bar{s}$	without
S.C. or subcut	subcutaneous
Sol	solution
sp	spirit
$\bar{ss}$	half
S.S.E.	soap solution enema
Stat	immediately
tab	tablet
T. or tbsp	tablespoon
t.i.d	three times a day
tinct. or tr	tincture
t. or tsp	teaspoon
U	unit

4. LABORATORY/X-RAY

AFB	acid fast bacillus
Ba.E	barium enema
BMR	basal metabolic rate
BSP	bromsulphalein
BUN	blood urea nitrogen
CBC	complete blood count
CO_2 vol.%	carbon dioxide volume
C and S	culture and sensitivity
Diff	differential count
ECG or EKG	electrocardiogram
EEG	electroencephalogram
FBS	fasting blood sugar
GB	gallbladder
GI	gastrointestinal
GTT	glucose tolerance test
hbg	hemoglobin
IVP	intravenous pyelogram
Lab	laboratory
NPN	non protéine nitrogène
P.B.I	protein bound iodine
P.P.D	purified protein derivative
PSP	phenolsulfonphthalein
R and M	routine and microscopic
RBC	red blood count
Sed.rate	sedimentation rate
spec	specimen
sp.gr	specific gravity

GLOSSARY OF MEDICAL TERMS (EYE, EAR, NOSE AND THROAT)

CONTENTS

	PAGE
ABDUCT ...... AUDIOMETER	1
AUDITORY CORTEX ...... COMPLAINT	2
COMPRESSION ...... EPITHELIUM	3
EQUILIBRIUM ...... FURUNCLE	4
GUSTATORY ...... INTRINSIC	5
LACERATION ...... MILLIMETER	6
MOLECULAR ...... OSTEOMYELITIS	7
OTOLARYNGOLOGIST ...... PSYCHIATRIC	8
PULMONARY ...... SPECULUM	9
SPHINCTER ...... TRAUMA	10
TRISMUS ...... VOCALIZATION	11

GLOSSARY OF MEDICAL TERMS (EYE, EAR, NOSE AND THROAT)

<u>A</u>

ABDUCT
  To draw away from the median line. When the vocal cords abduct, they separate.
ACCELERATION
  A quickening or speeding up.
ACOUSTIC
  As pertaining to sound or to the sense of hearing.
ACUTE
  Having a short and relatively severe course.
ADDUCT
  To move towards the median. When the vocal cords adduct, they come together.
ADENOIDITIS
  Inflammation of the adenoid tissue in the nasopharynx.
ALLERGEN
  The material responsible for an allergic reaction.
AMPLIFY
  The process of making larger or louder, as the increase of an auditory stimulus.
ANATOMY
  The science of the structure of the body and the relation of its parts.
ANGINA
  A severe pain.
ANGULAR
  Sharply bent; having corners or angles.
ANTIBIOTIC
  A chemical substance which has the capacity to inhibit the growth of or destroy bacteria and other microorganisms.
ANTIHISTAMINE
  Any of several drugs used to minimize an allergic reaction.
ANTISEPTIC
  A substance that will inhibit the growth and development of microorganisms.
ASCENT
  A rising up. The amount of upward slope or elevation.
ASEPTIC
  Not septic. Free from infectious material.
ASPIRATION
  The removal of fluids or debris from a cavity by means of an aspirator.
ASTHMA
  A disease marked by recurrent attacks of difficult breathing.
ATMOSPHERIC PRESSURE
  The pressure due to the weight of the earth's atmosphere, equal at sea level to about 14.7 pounds per square inch.
AUDIOMETER
  Device for testing the power of hearing.

AUDITORY CORTEX
   The sensory area of hearing located in the temporal lobe of the brain.
AURICLE
   That portion of the external ear not contained within the head.
AUTOCLAVE
   An apparatus for effecting sterilization by steam under pressure.

B

BACTERIA
   A loosely used generic name for any microorganism of the order Eubacteriales.
BACTERIAL
   Pertaining to or caused by bacteria.
BAROTRAUMA
   Injury caused by pressure, such as injury to the middle ear or sinus cavity due to difference in pressure between the atmosphere and the inside of the cavity.
BENIGN
   Not malignant.
BIFID
   Clefts into two parts or branches.
BILATERAL
   Having two sides or pertaining to two layers.

C

CANNULATION
   The insertion of a cannula into a hollow organ or body cavity.
CAUTERIZE
   To burn with a hot instrument or with a caustic substance so as to destroy tissue or prevent the spread of infection.
CELLULITIS
   Infection or inflammation of the loose subcutaneous tissue.
CENTIMETER
   A unit of measurement in the metric system. Being equal to 0.3937 inch.
CEREBRAL SPINAL FLUID
   A clear fluid contained within the cavities of and surrounding the brain and spinal cord.
CERUMEN
   The wax-like secretion found within the external auditory canal.
CHONDROMA
   A benign tumor of cartilage.
CHRONIC
   Persisting over a long period of time.
COMMINUTION
   Broken into small fragments.
COMPLAINT
   The symptom or group of symptoms about which the patient consults the physician.

COMPRESSION
  The act of pressing together to diminish volume and increase density.
CONCOMITANT
  Accompanying or joined with another.
CONGENITAL
  Existing at or before birth.
CULTURE
  The propagation of microorganisms in a special media.
CURRETAGE
  To remove by scraping.
CYCLES PER SECOND
  In audiology, the number of sound waves passing a point per second.
CYST
  A sac which contains a liquid or semisolid material.

D

DECAY
  The process of stage of decline. The decomposition of dead organic matter.
DECONGESTANT
  A drug which reduces congestion or swelling.
DEMARKATION
  Any dividing line apparent on the surface of the body, such as the boundary between normal and infected tissue.
DERMATITIS
  Inflammation of the skin.
DESCENT
  A coming down, going down, or downward motion.
DIPLOPIA
  Double vision.
DISCRIMINATION
  The ability to make or to perceive distinctions.

E

EDEMA
  The presence of abnormally large amounts of fluid in the intercellular tissue spaces of the body.
ENDOLYMPH
  The fluid contained in the membranous labyrinth of the ear.
ENOPHTHALMUS
  Abnormal retraction of the eye into the orbit.
ENTITY
  An independently existing thing; a reality.
EPISTAXIS
  Nose bleed or hemorrhage from the nose.
EPITHELIUM
  The covering of the internal and external surfaces of the body.

EQUILIBRIUM
A state of balance. A condition in which opposing forces exactly counteract each other.

ERYTHEMA
A name applied to redness of the skin produced by congestion of the capillaries. This may result in a variety of causes such as infection and trauma.

EUSTACHIAN TUBE
A slender tube between the middle ear and the pharynx which serves to equalize air pressure on both sides of the ear drum. Named after Bartolommeo Eustachio, an Italian anatomist.

EVACUATE
To make empty; to remove the contents.

EXACERBATION
An increase or recurrence in the severity of any symptom or disease.

EXCISION
An act of removing by cutting away.

EXOSTOSIS
An abnormal bony protuberance.

EXTRINSIC
Coming from or originating outside the organ or limb where found.

EXUDATE
Material such as fluid, cells, or cellular debris which has been deposited in or on tissue surfaces. This usually is the result of inflammation.

F

FIBROUS
Composed of or containing fibers.

FILAMENTOUS
Long, thread-like structures.

FIXATION
The act of holding, suturing, or fastening in a fixed position. Direction of a gaze so that the image of the object looked at falls on the fovea centralis.

FORAMEN
A natural opening or passage, especially a passage into or through a bone.

FREQUENCY
The number of vibrations made by a particle or ray per unit of time.

FUNCTIONAL HEARING LOSS
Hearing loss without an organic basis, such as malingering or psychological.

FUNGUS
A class of vegetable organisms of a low order of development which includes molds, mushrooms, and toadstools.

FURUNCLE
A painful nodule formed in the skin by bacteria which enter into the hair follicles causing a localized infection.

G

GUSTATORY
  Pertaining to the sense of taste.

H

HEMATOMA
  A swelling containing blood.
HERTZ
  The international unit of frequency, equal to one cycle per second.
HIVES
  An allergic skin condition characterized by itching, burning, and stinging during the formation of a red papular rash.
HYPERACTIVE
  Abnormally increased activity.
HYPEREMIA
  Redness of a part due to engorgement of blood vessels.
HYPERTENSION
  Abnormally high blood pressure.
HYPERTROPHIC
  The enlargement or overgrowth of an organ due to an increase in size of its cells.
HYPERVENTILATION
  Abnormally rapid and deep breathing.
HYPOACTIVE
  Abnormally diminished activity.
HYSTERIA
  A psychoneurosis characterized by lack of control of emotions.

I

IMPREGNATE
  To saturate one material with another, such as to saturate gauze with an ointment.
INBIBITION
  The absorption of a liquid.
INCISION
  A cut or a wound produced by cutting.
INFECTION
  Invasion of the body by pathogenic microorganisms and the reaction of the tissue to their presence and to the toxins generated by the microorganisms.
INFLAMMATION
  The condition into which tissues enter as a reaction to injury or infection. It is characterized by pain, heat, redness, and swelling of the area.
INTRINSIC
  Situated entirely within or pertaining exclusively to a part.

L

LACERATION
A wound made by tearing.

LARYNGITIS
Inflammation of the larynx.

LARYNGOPHARYNX
That portion of the pharynx lying between the upper edge of the epiglottis and the vocal cords.

LATENT
Concealed or not yet manifest.

LATERAL
The position of a part further from midline than another part of the same side.

LESION
A pathologic or traumatic lack of continuity of tissue or loss of function of a part.

LEUKEMIA
A fatal disease of the blood-forming organs characterized by a marked increase in the number of white blood cells.

LINEAR
Pertaining to or resembling a line. Linear acceleration means acceleration in a straight line.

M

MALAISE
A vague feeling of discomfort.

MALIGNANT
As applied to tumors, malignant means the tendency to invade surrounding structures and the ability to spread to other parts of the body by way of the bloodstream or lymphatic channels.

MALINGERING
The faking or exaggeration of symptoms of an illness or injury.

MALOCCLUSION
The lack of occlusion between the maxillary and mandibular teeth which interferes with mastication.

MANIFEST
Something which is readily evident or clear to the sight or mind.

MARSUPIALIZATION
An operation which removes a portion of a cyst, abscess, or tumor, empties its contents, and sutures its edges to the line of incision.

MASTICATION
The chewing of food.

MEMBRANE
A layer of tissue which covers the surface or divides a space or organ.

MENINGITIS
An inflammation or infection of the meningeal covering of the brain.

MICRON
A unit of measurement equal to 1/1000th of a millimeter.

MILLIMETER
A unit of measurement equaling 1/1000th of a meter or 0.03937 inch.

MOLECULAR
  Pertaining to molecules or a chemical combination of two or more atoms.
MORBIDITY
  The condition of being diseased or sick.
MORTALITY
  Death.
MUCOSA
  The mucous membrane covering a surface such as the membrane covering the surface of the palate or tongue.
MYRINGITIS
  Inflammation of the tympanic membrane.
MYRINGOTOMY
  An incision through the tympanic membrane.
MYRINGOPLASTY
  The surgical repair of a perforation in the tympanic membrane.

N

NECROSIS
  The death of a tissue or a part.
NEOPLASM
  Any new growth or tumor. It may be either a benign or malignant process.
NYSTAGMUS
  An involuntary rapid movement of the eyeball which may be horizontal, vertical, or rotary.

O

OBJECTIVE
  Pertaining to things which are perceptible to the senses.
OCCLUSION
  The relationship of the maxillary and mandibular teeth when in functional contact.
OINTMENT
  A semisolid preparation for external application to the body.
OLFACTION
  The sense of smell or the act of smelling.
OMINOUS
  Serving as an omen, or having a character of an evil omen.
OPEN REDUCTION
  Reduction of a fracture after exposing the fracture by an incision.
ORGANISM
  A body of living material. It may be a single cell, plant, or animal.
ORIFICE
  The entrance or outlet of any body cavity.
OSSEOUS
  Bone or bony.
OSTEOMYELITIS
  Inflammation or infection of bone.

OTOLARYNGOLOGIST
A physician who has specialized in the surgical and medical treatment of diseases of the ear, nose, and throat.

OTORRHEA
A discharge from the ear.

OTOTOXIC
Pertaining to something which is toxic to the ear. Specifically, certain drugs destroy the minute sensory cells of the inner ear.

P

PARENTERAL
Refers to medicine given by the subcutaneous, intramuscular, or intravenous route.

PARESIS
Slight or incomplete paralysis.

PATENT
Open, unobstructed.

PATHOGENIC
Refers to an organism or substance capable of causing disease.

PEDIATRIC
That branch of medicine which treats children.

PERCEPTION
The awareness of objects or other data through the medium of the senses.

PERFORATE
To pierce with holes.

PERIPHERY
Away from center. Example: The finger is peripheral to the elbow.

PETROUS
Resembling a rock. The petrous bone is so-called because of its hardness.

PHARYNGITIS
Inflammation of the pharynx.

PHARYNX
The tube between the posterior portion of the mouth and nose above, and the trachea and esophagus below.

PRACTITIONER
An authorized practitioner of medicine.

PHYSIOLOGY
The science or study of the function of living organisms.

PITCH
The quality of sound dependent upon the frequency of vibration.

PNEUMATIZATION
The formation of air-filled cells or cavities in tissues. Especially such formation in the temporal bone.

PROPAGATE
To reproduce, multiply, or spread.

PROPHYLACTIC
An agent that tends to ward off disease.

PSYCHIATRIC
That branch of medicine which deals with disorders of the human mind.

PULMONARY
  Pertaining to the lungs.
PURULENT
  Consists of or contains pus.

Q

QUALITATIVE
  Having to do with the quality of something.
QUANTITATIVE
  Having to do with the quantity of something, capable of being measured.

R

RAPPORT
  A close or sympathetic relationship.
RAREFACTION
  The condition of being or becoming less dense.
REVOLUTION
  A turning or spinning motion of a body or thing around a center axis.
RHINORRHEA
  The discharge of material from the nose.
RHINOSCOPY
  The examination of the nasal passages.
ROENTGENOGRAM
  The film produced by x-ray.

S

SALINE
  A solution of salt and water.
SALPINGITIS
  Inflammation of a tube. For example: eustachian salpingitis.
SAPROPHYTE
  An organism that lives on dead or decaying organic matter.
SEBACEOUS GLANDS
  Glands which secrete a greasy lubricating substance.
SEPTOPLASTY
  An operation to straighten the nasoseptum.
SEROUS
  Material which resembles blood serum.
SIMPLE FRACTURE
  A fracture of bone in which the bone does not protrude through the skin.
SPECULUM
  An appliance used to view a passage or cavity in the body. Examples include nasal and ear speculums.

SPHINCTER
  A ring-like band of muscle fibers that constrict a passage or close a natural orifice.
SPONDEE
  Two heavily accented syllables.
SPONTANEOUS
  Occurring without external influence. Such as the spontaneous recovery from an illness.
STAPEDECTOMY
  An operation which includes the removal of the stapes and its footplate, and placement of some form of prosthesis, such as wire, to take the place of the stapes.
STEROID
  A group of compounds that resemble cholesterol. For the most part, these drugs are used for their anti-inflammatory effect. Cortisone is the best known example of this group of medications.
STIMULUS
  Any agent, act, or influence that produces a reaction in the receptor.
STOMATITIS
  Inflammation of the oral mucosa.
STRIDOR
  The wheezing noise present on inspiration or expiration when partial obstruction of the larynx is present.
SUBCUTANEOUS
  Situated or occurring beneath the skin.
SUBEPITHELIAL
  Situated beneath the epithelium.
SUBJECTIVE
  Pertaining to or perceived only by the affected individual.
SUBMUCOUS RESECTION
  Excision of the cartilage of the nasoseptum.
SUPINE
  The position assumed when lying on the back.
SYMPTOM
  Any change in a patient's condition indicative of some bodily or mental state.
SYSTEMIC
  Pertaining to or affecting the body as a whole.

T

THERMAL
  Pertaining to, characterized by heat.
THRESHOLD
  That value at which a stimulus minimally produces a sensation.
TINNITUS
  A buzzing or ringing noise in the ears.
TRANSUDATE
  A fluid substance which has passed through a membrane or has been extruded from a tissue as a result of inflammation.
TRAUMA
  A wound or injury.

TRISMUS
Difficulty in opening the mouth due to mascular spasms, pain, or disturbance of the 5th cranial nerve.

TUMOR
Any swelling. It may indicate either inflammation, infection, or neoplasm.

TYMPANOPLASTY
Surgical reconstruction of the hearing mechanism of the middle ear.

U

UNILATERAL
Affecting one side only.

V

VENEREAL
Due to or propagated by sexual intercourse.

VERTIGO
A hallucination of movement. A sensation as if the external environment is revolving around the patient, or as if the patient were revolving in space.

VESICULATION
Small circumscribed elevations of epithelium containing a serous liquid.

VIRUS
One of a group of minute infectious agents which are too small to be seen under a microscope.

VOCALIZATION
The act of making a sound through the mouth.

www.ingramcontent.com/pod-product-compliance
Lightning Source LLC
Chambersburg PA
CBHW080737230426
43665CB00020B/2771